Bilingual Course of Exercise Biochemistry

运动生物化学双语教程

严翊　梁春瑜　编著

北京体育大学出版社

策划编辑　佟　晖
责任编辑　佟　晖
责任校对　潘海英
版式设计　联众恒创

图书在版编目（CIP）数据

运动生物化学双语教程 = Bilingual Course of
Exercise Biochemistry：汉、英 / 严翊 , 梁春瑜编著
. -- 北京：北京体育大学出版社 , 2024.12
　　ISBN 978-7-5644-4103-6

　　Ⅰ . ①运… Ⅱ . ①严… ②梁… Ⅲ . ①运动生物化学
—教材—汉、英 Ⅳ . ① G804.7

中国国家版本馆 CIP 数据核字 (2024) 第 107433 号

运动生物化学双语教程
YUNDONG SHENGWU HUAXUE SHUANGYU JIAOCHENG

严翊　梁春瑜　编著

出版发行：北京体育大学出版社
地　　址：北京市海淀区农大南路 1 号院 2 号楼 2 层办公 B-212
邮　　编：100084
网　　址：http://cbs. bsu. edu. cn
发 行 部：010-62989320
邮 购 部：北京体育大学出版社读者服务部 010-62989432
印　　刷：北京科信印刷有限公司
开　　本：787mm×1092mm　1/16
成品尺寸：185mm×260mm
印　　张：9.5
字　　数：244 千字
版　　次：2024 年 12 月第 1 版
印　　次：2024 年 12 月第 1 次印刷
定　　价：60.00 元

CONTENTS

Part III Exercise and Health

目录

Part I The Biological Substances Basics for Exercise

第一篇　人体运动的物质基础

○ **Learning Objectives**

· Distinguish the classifications of carbohydrates, lipids, proteins, vitamins and minerals.
· Outline the digestion processes and storage forms of carbohydrates, lipids, proteins, vitamins, minerals and water.
· Describe the biological functions of carbohydrates, lipids, proteins, vitamins, minerals and water.

○ **学习目标**

· 掌握糖类、脂类、蛋白质、维生素、矿物质的分类。
· 了解糖类、脂类、蛋白质、维生素、矿物质、水的消化吸收过程及储存形式。
· 掌握糖类、脂类、蛋白质、维生素、矿物质、水的生物学功能。

The biological substances that all living organism needs can be divided into the organic substances and inorganic substances. In order to synthesize these biological substances, which is necessary to maintain metabolism and life, the human body needs to obtain nutrients from food, including carbohydrates, fats, proteins, vitamins, minerals and water. The organic process by which organisms absorb nutrients from food and use them to provide energy, to supply raw materials for tissues building, and to regulate body functions, is called nutrition. Among these nutrients, carbohydrate, fat, and protein are classified as macronutrients. They provide all the energy that body needs, because the body consumes hundreds of grams of these every day. In contrast, vitamin and mineral are known as micronutrients because the body consumes only a few grams or even less than a gram. Water does not fall into any of these categories, because the human body needs much more water than any macronutrient in daily life.

Since the nutrients provide energy and regulate physiologic processes during exercise, exercise performance and various biological responses to exercise depend on the quantity and type of food and dietary supplements a person consumes. Such improved athletic performances are linked with dietary adaptation and optimization. This section will introduce the composition, functions and sources of each nutrient (carbohydrate, lipid, protein, vitamin, mineral, and water), and explore the roles they play in exercise.

生物体所需要的生物物质包括有机物和无机物。为了合成维持新陈代谢和生命所必需的生物物质，人体需要从食物中获取营养素，如糖类、脂类、蛋白质、维生素、矿物质和水。有机体吸收食物中的营养素并将其用于提供能量、提供组织构建的原材料和调节身体功能的生物学过程就是营养。在营养物质中，机体每天对糖类、脂类和蛋白质的需要量在数百克，因此这些营养素被称为宏量营养素，它们能够提供人体所需的所有能量。相比之下，维生素和矿物质被称为微量营养素，因为人体每天对维生素和矿物质的需要量只有几克甚至不到一克。水不属于任何一类，因为人体对水的需求量比任何宏量营养素都要大得多。

因为营养素可以在运动中提供能量并调节生理代谢过程，所以运动表现和运动引起的许多生物效应与一个人摄入的食物和膳食补充剂的数量及种类密切相关。运动成绩的提高往往与饮食的调整和优化有关。本篇将重点介绍各种营养素（糖类、脂类、蛋白质、维生素、矿物质和水）的组成、功能和来源，并探讨它们在运动中的作用。

Chapter 1   Carbohydrates

第一章　糖　类

Saccharides are the most abundant organic molecules in nature, and consist of carbon, hydrogen and oxygen. Certain simpler saccharides have the general formula $C_n(H_2O)_n$, so saccharides are commonly called hydrates of carbon (carbohydrates). In fact, not all the saccharides have the molecular formula of $C_n(H_2O)_n$, such as deoxyribose ($C_5H_{10}O_4$); there are some substances with the chemical formula of $C_n(H_2O)_n$ that are not saccharides, such as lactic acid [$C_3(H_2O)_3$], but they are still called carbohydrates.

There seems to be a relationship between dietary carbohydrates and blood glucose, muscle glycogen content, which are important factors that affect exercise performance. Therefore, it is necessary to have a deeper understanding of the biochemistry of carbohydrates.

由碳、氢、氧元素组成的糖类是自然界中含量最丰富的有机分子。由于某些简单的糖类的结构通式可以写成 $C_n（H_2O）_n$，因此糖类又被称为碳水化合物。虽然实际上并不是所有的糖类的结构式都符合 $C_n（H_2O）_n$ 的分子式，例如脱氧核糖（$C_5H_{10}O_4$）；符合 $C_n（H_2O）_n$ 分子式的物质也并不都属于糖类，例如乳酸［$C_3（H_2O）_3$］，但是人们仍然习惯将糖类称为碳水化合物。

血糖、肌糖原是影响运动表现的重要因素，食物中糖类的摄入量与血糖、肌糖原含量密切相关。因此，深入了解糖类的生物化学特性是至关重要的。

1.1 Classification and Sources of Carbohydrates
糖类的分类及来源

Carbohydrates are divided into simple and complex carbohydrates in nutritional terms. However, biochemists divide carbohydrates into three general groups: monosaccharides, oligosaccharides, and polysaccharides. Except for lactose and a small amount of glycogen from animal origins, the majority of carbohydrate forms are derived from plants.

从营养学角度，可以将糖类分为简单糖类和复杂糖类。但从生物化学的角度，可以将糖类分为单糖、低聚糖和多糖三大类。除了乳糖和少量动物来源的糖原，大多数的糖类来源于植物。

1.1.1 Monosaccharides
单糖

Monosaccharides, with carbon atoms normally ranging from 3 to 7, are the simplest carbohydrates, and they are the basic unit of carbohydrates. Monosaccharides are the only form that can be absorbed by the body. Therefore, all form carbohydrates must be digested into monosaccharides before they can be absorbed by the body. Glucose, fructose and galactose are three types of monosaccharides that possess significant nutritional value, and they are isomers of each other (Figure 1.1).

单糖是最简单的糖，所含碳原子数量一般是 3~7 个。单糖是糖类的基本单位。单糖作为人体可直接吸收的唯一糖类形式。因此，无论何种形式的糖类，都需经过消化分解为单糖才能被人体吸收。葡萄糖、果糖和半乳糖是三种重要的营养单糖，它们互为异构体（图 1.1）。

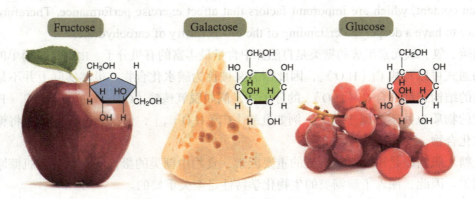

Figure 1.1　The molecular structure of glucose, fructose and galactose

Glucose is the preferred fuel used by the body and the most prevalent carbohydrate form found in the body. After glucose is absorbed by the small intestine, it can　① turn into blood glucose, serving as an energy source for cellular metabolism and trigger the insulin response; ② be stored as glycogen in the liver and muscles; or ③ be converted into fat (triacylglycerol) for later use as energy.

Fructose, the sweetest sugar, is found abundantly in fruits and honey. Some fructose enters blood directly from the digestive tract and does not trigger the release of insulin, while all fructose will eventually be converted to glucose or fat (triacylglycerol) stored in the liver tissue. More and more evidence show that fructose intake is closely associated with obesity and liver disease, so more attention should be paid to the health effects of excessive fructose consumption.

Galactose is not found in its free form in nature, as it only occurs in a combined state. It either comes from dietary sources (milk, sugar beets, etc.) or is produced in the body. The body can use galactose in building glycolipids and glycoproteins in some circumstance, or convert galactose into glucose for energy metabolism.

Ribose is another type of biological monosaccharides, but it have no nutritional or caloric value to the body.

葡萄糖是人体首选的燃料，也是人体中最常见的糖。葡萄糖被小肠吸收后，可以①成为血糖，作为细胞代谢的能量来源，触发胰岛素反应；②形成糖原储存在肝脏和肌肉中；③转化为脂肪（甘油三酯），储存能量供以后使用。

果糖是最甜的糖，大量存在于水果和蜂蜜中。有些果糖可以直接从消化道进入血液，而不引起胰岛素释放，但最终都会转化成葡萄糖或脂肪（甘油三酯）并储存在肝脏组织中。越来越多的证据显示，果糖的摄入与肥胖和肝脏疾病之间存在密切的相关性。因此，关注果糖摄入过量对健康的影响是非常有必要的。

半乳糖在自然界中不以游离态存在，而仅以化合态形式出现。它通常来自于食物（如牛奶和甜菜），或者是在体内合成。人体在一定程度上可以利用半乳糖合成糖脂和糖蛋白，或将半乳糖转化为葡萄糖用于能量代谢。

核糖是另一类生物单糖，它们对身体没有真正的营养或热量价值。

1.1.2 Oligosaccharides

低聚糖

Oligosaccharides refers to saccharides with 2–10 monosaccharides linked by glycosidic bonds. For example, when two monosaccharide molecules are combined, a disaccharide is formed.

Sucrose (a combination of one glucose and one fructose molecule), lactose (a combination of one glucose and one galactose molecule) and maltose (a combination of two glucose molecules) are three types of disaccharides with important nutritional value (Figure 1.2). They are generally converted to glucose for fuel or storage.

低聚糖是由2~10个单糖通过糖苷键连接而成的。例如，两个单糖分子结合可形成双糖。

乳糖（由一个葡萄糖和一种半乳糖分子组合而成）、麦芽糖（由两个葡萄糖分子组合而成）和蔗糖（由一个葡萄糖和一个果糖分子组合而成）是三种发挥重要营养作用的双糖（图 1.2）。它们都可以转化成葡萄糖而发挥燃料的作用或被储存。

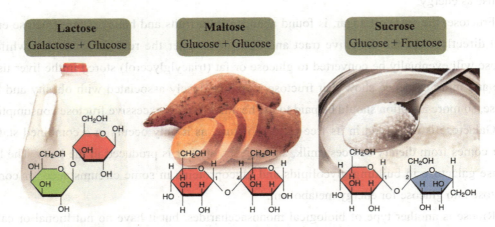

Figure 1.2　The molecular structure of lactose, maltose and sucrose

1.1.3 Polysaccharides
多糖

Polysaccharides contain more than ten, sometimes even thousands of monosaccharide residues. The monosaccharides that compose polysaccharides can be the same (homopolysaccharides) or different (heteropolysaccharides) monosaccharides.

Starch, fiber, and glycogen, as three common forms of homopolysaccharides, are composed of glucose. Starch and fiber are the storage forms of carbohydrate in plants, such as grains, beans, fruits and vegetables. There are two forms of starch, amylose and amylopectin (Figure 1.3). Starches with relatively a large amount of amylopectin are digested and absorbed rapidly, while starches with high amylose content break down (hydrolyze) at a slower rate.

多糖中含有 10 个以上甚至数千个单糖残基，是糖类中含量最丰富的一类。组成多糖的单糖可以是同一种单糖（同多糖），也可以是不同种的单糖（杂多糖）。

淀粉、纤维素和糖原是由葡萄糖组成的三种常见的同多糖。淀粉和纤维素是植物中糖类的储存形式，如谷物、豆类、水果和蔬菜。淀粉有直链淀粉和支链淀粉两种形式（图 1.3）。支链淀粉含量较高的淀粉消化和吸收较快，而直链淀粉含量较高的淀粉分解（水解）速度较慢。

Fiber, classified as soluble and insoluble, cannot be broken down by human digestive enzymes, so it cannot be absorbed well. But it still plays an important role in maintaining the health of the digestive system, such as reducing food intake by providing a feeling of fullness in the stomach, helping to maintain stable blood glucose levels, improving intestinal health, preventing constipation, and reducing the absorption of fat and cholesterol.

Glycogen, stored mainly in the muscles and liver of mammals, is crucial for energy metabolism. Glycogen is similar in structure to amylopectin, and it is also called animal starch. Glycogen appears to have more branches (8 to 12 glucose residues) and shorter chains (12 to 14 glucose residues), so as to break down faster and holds a prominent position in exercise metabolism.

Figure 1.3   The molecular structure of amylose, amylopectin and fiber

纤维素分为可溶性纤维素和非可溶性纤维素两类。由于不能被人体消化酶分解，因此纤维素不能被很好地吸收，但它在维持消化系统健康方面仍然发挥着重要的作用。例如，纤维素可以通过提供饱腹感来减少食物摄入，并有助于维持稳定的血糖水平，改善肠道健康，防止便秘。纤维素还可以减少脂肪和胆固醇的吸收。

糖原主要储存在哺乳动物的肌肉和肝脏中，对能量代谢至关重要。糖原在结构上与支链淀粉相似，又被称为动物淀粉。糖原的分支数量更多（每隔 8~12 个葡萄糖残基形成一个分支），长度更短（含有 12~14 个葡萄糖残基），因此分解得更快，在运动代谢中具有突出地位。

1.2 Digestion of Carbohydrates
糖类的消化吸收

Most of the carbohydrates in the daily diet are starch, which is digested in the mouth and intestinal lumen respectively by amylase released from salivary glands, pancreatic amylase and other enzymes in the gastrointestinal tract. The final products of dietary carbohydrate digestion are monosaccharides, such as glucose, galactose, and fructose. They are absorbed through the lining of the small intestine and then transported to the portal vein. This vein is the main supplier of blood to the liver, which serves as the distribution center of carbohydrates for the entire body. Once the liver receives dietary monosaccharides from the portal vein, the portion of monosaccharides is used to synthesize the glycogen, and the rest is released into the bloodstream, and transported to all other tissues of the body (Figure 1.4).

淀粉是食物中主要的糖类，经过口腔中唾液腺释放的淀粉酶、肠腔释放的胰淀粉酶，以及胃肠道的其他酶的消化后，最终分解成单糖，如葡萄糖、半乳糖和果糖。这些单糖通过小肠内壁被吸收并最终运输到门静脉。门静脉是肝脏血液的主要供给者，而肝脏又是全身的糖类分配中心。一旦肝脏从门静脉接收到食物来源的单糖，它就会保留一部分主要用于合成糖原，并将其余的部分释放到血液中，再运送到全身各个组织（图 1.4）。

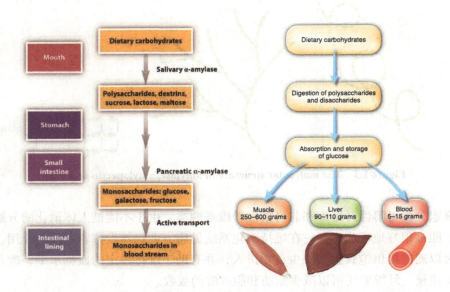

Figure 1.4   The digestion and storage of carbohydrate

All carbohydrates and carbohydrate-containing foods are not digested and absorbed at a similar rate. The glycemic index (GI) of food is an indicator of how rapidly blood glucose levels rise in 2 hours after consumption of the food containing 50g of carbohydrate. The glucose that enters the blood is called blood glucose (blood sugar), which will result in the increase in the blood glucose level after ingestion. Glucose is considered the standard and assigned the GI value of 100. When measured according to the rate of glucose, the scoring system categorizes carbohydrates as high-glycemic foods (score:100 to 70), medium-glycemic foods (score: 69 to 56), or low-glycemic foods (score: 55 to 0) (Figure 1.5).

Because of the different sites of digestion and absorption in the intestinal tract, foods with low GI have a slower absorption rate and a smaller blood sugar fluctuation range than foods with high GI. Thus, foods with low GI are much more beneficial to maintain the stability of blood sugar level for a long time (Figure 1.6). High GI foods are generally not recommended but after a prolonged exercise, foods with medium to high-GI offer more benefits for the rapid replenishment of carbohydrates than low GI foods.

Due to the lack of lactase required for breaking down lactose into glucose and galactose, some individuals may suffer from a variety of gastrointestinal disorders such as diarrhea when they consume dairy products. This is called "lactose intolerance". Over 60% of adults in the world suffer from lactose intolerance.

各种糖类和含糖的食物消化和吸收的速率都不相同。食物的升糖指数（glycemic index，GI）是反映摄入含有 50 g 糖类的食物后 2 h 内的血糖浓度升高的速度快慢的指标。进入血液的葡萄糖称为血糖，因此进食葡萄糖后的血糖浓度升高的速度是最快的，以此为标准，设定葡萄糖的升糖指数为 100。与葡萄糖的升糖速度相比，可将含糖食物分为高升糖指数食物（GI：100~70 分）、中升糖指数食物（GI：69~56 分）和低升糖指数食物（GI：55~0 分）（图 1.5）。

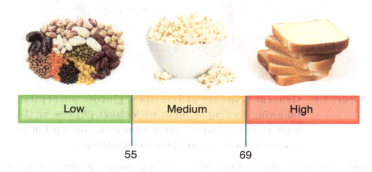

Figure 1.5   Cutoff values of low, medium, and high glycemic index foods

如图 1.6 所示，由于在肠道内消化吸收的部位不同，低 GI 食物比高 GI 食物吸收得慢，引起的血糖波动幅度小，更有利于长时间维持血糖水平的稳定。所以，一般不推荐食用高 GI 的食物。但在长时间运动后，中到高 GI 的食物比低 GI 的食物更有利于快速补充糖类。

由于缺乏将乳糖分解为葡萄糖和半乳糖所需的乳糖酶，一些人在食用乳制品时可能会出现腹泻等各种胃肠道不良反应，这种现象称为"乳糖不耐受症"。超过 60% 的成年人有乳糖不耐受症。

1.3 Storage of Carbohydrates
糖类的储存

Once carbohydrates enter the body, they are either used as a direct energy source or transported to cells for storage as glycogen. In the body, carbohydrates are generally stored in the blood as blood glucose (5–15 g), in the liver as liver glycogen (90–110 g, 3% to 7% of the liver weight) and in the muscle as muscle glycogen (250–600 g, 1% to 1.5% of the muscle weight) (Figure 1.4).

Blood glucose (blood sugar) is the direct fuel of the body and utilized by all tissues.

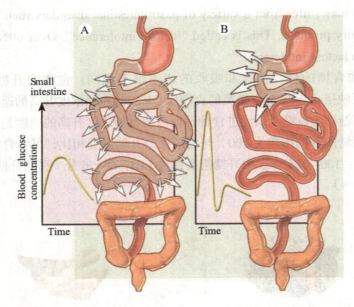

Figure 1.6   General response of intestinal glucose absorption following feeding of foods with either (A) low or (B) high glycemic index. Arrows indicate absorption of glucose from the areas of the small intestine

Especially the brain, neural system and red blood cells depend on glucose as their primary fuel. The brain accounts for 2% of the human body weight but uses 25% of the total blood glucose. Red blood cells lack mitochondria, so anaerobic glycolysis of glucose is their unique energy source. Maintaining normal blood glucose levels (fasting:3.92–6.16 mmol/L) primarily depends on liver glycogenolysis, but not muscle glycogen. When the fasting blood glucose in healthy adults is lower than 2.8 mmol/L (below 3.9 mmol/L in diabetic patients), hypoglycemia will occur and the clinical symptoms are weakness, hunger, mental confusion, and dizziness. Sustained and profound hypoglycemia may trigger unconsciousness and result in irreversible brain damage.

　　糖类一旦进入机体后，可以作为直接供能物质被利用，也可以被运输到细胞中作为糖原储存。机体内的糖类通常在血液中以血糖（5~15 g）的形式存在，或者在肝脏和肌肉中分别以肝糖原（90~110 g，约占肝脏重量的 3%~7%）、肌糖原（250~600 g，占肌肉重量的 1%~1.5%）的形式存在。（图 1.4）

　　血糖是身体的直接燃料，可以被全身各个组织利用。特别是大脑、神经组织和红细胞都依赖于葡萄糖作为它们的主要燃料。大脑占人体体重的 2%，其消耗的血糖可占血糖总量的 25%。红细胞缺少线粒体，所以葡萄糖的无氧糖酵解是它们唯一的能量来源。维持正常的血糖水平（空腹血糖：3.92~6.16 mmol/L），主要依赖肝糖原的分解，而不是肌糖原。健康成人空腹血糖低于 2.8mmol/L（糖尿病血糖低于 3.9 mmol/L）时，出现低血糖，临床表现为虚弱、饥饿、精神错乱、头晕。持续和严重的低血糖会导致意识丧失，并产生不可逆转的脑损伤。

Insulin and glucagon released from the pancreas are the main hormones regulating the blood glucose level. After a typical high-carbohydrate meal, insulin is released into the blood and promotes the transport of dietary glucose into cells for utilization or storage, thereby decreasing blood glucose to the normal level. In contrast, glucagon promotes the liver glycogen decomposition to increase the blood glucose level.

Liver glycogen and muscle glycogen are found in the cytosol of hepatocytes (liver cells) and muscle fibers respectively in the form of granules. An 80 kg healthy man can store up to 400 g of muscle glycogen and 110 g of liver glycogen. In the liver, glycogen serves as a source of blood glucose. In muscles, glycogen serves as a fuel source for the generation of ATP. Both liver and muscle glycogen are influenced by diet and exercise (Table 1.1). For example, a 24-hour fast or a low-carbohydrate diet can nearly deplete glycogen stores. In contrast, compared with a typical balanced diet, a few days of a carbohydrate-rich diet almost doubles the body's carbohydrate storage, which is good for improving exercise performance. In the resting state, fasting has little influence on the muscle glycogen storage.

胰腺释放的胰岛素和胰高血糖素是调节血糖水平的主要激素。在典型的高糖膳食后，胰岛素被释放到血液中，促进饮食中的葡萄糖被运输到细胞中利用和储存，从而使血糖降至正常水平。而胰高血糖素则促进肝糖原分解，提高血糖水平。

肝糖原和肌糖原以颗粒的形式分别存在于肝细胞的胞浆和肌肉的肌纤维之间。一个健康的 80 kg 的男性，最多可以储存约 400 g 的肌糖原和 110 g 的肝糖原。在肝脏中，储存的糖原是血糖的来源；在肌肉中，储存的糖原是产生 ATP 的燃料来源。肝糖原和肌糖原含量均受饮食和运动的影响（表 1.1）。例如，24 h 的禁食或低糖饮食几乎会耗尽糖原储备。相比之下，几天的高糖饮食可以使体内糖储备比典型的平衡饮食增加几乎一倍，这有利于提高运动成绩。安静状态下，禁食对肌糖原储量的影响很少。

1.4 Biological Function of Carbohydrates
糖类的生物学功能

Carbohydrates have various functions within the body. First, as one of the three important energy sources, carbohydrates provide energy for many organs. Certain organs and tissues, such as the brain, central nervous system, red blood cells and working muscles, require continuous supply of glucose as the metabolic fuel. In addition, an adequate supply of carbohydrate helps to inhibit the breakdown of protein as the energy source. Second, carbohydrates act as a storage form of energy in the blood, liver and muscles. And any additional carbohydrates will be converted to fats. Third, carbohydrates, serving as cell membrane components, can mediate certain types of intercellular communication. Finally, carbohydrates are also considered as "fat primer", because the complete catabolism of fats requires the participation of carbohydrates.

Table 1.1 Regulation of Liver and Muscle Glycogen Storage

Tissue	State	Regulater	Response of Tissue
Liver	Fasting	Blood: glucagon ↑ Insulin ↓ Tissue: cAMP ↑	Glycogen degradation ↑ Glycogen synthesis ↓
	Carbohydrate meal	Blood: glucagon ↓ Insulin ↑ Glucose ↑ Tissue: cAMP ↓ Glucose ↑	Glycogen degradation ↓ Glycogen synthesis ↑
	Exercise and stress	Blood: epinephrine ↑ Tissue: cAMP ↑ Ca^{2+}-calmodulin ↑	Glycogen degradation ↑ Glycogen synthesis ↓
Muscle	Fasting (rest)	Blood: insulin ↓	Glycogen synthesis ↓ Glucose transport ↓
	Carbohydrate meal (rest)	Blood: insulin ↑	Glycogen synthesis ↑ Glucose transport ↑
	Exercise and stress	Blood: epinephrine ↑ Tissue: AMP ↑ Ca^{2+}-calmodulin ↑ cAMP ↑	Glycogen synthesis ↓ Glycogen degradation ↑ Glycolysis ↑

　　糖类具有多种生物学功能。首先，糖类作为三种重要的能量来源之一，可以为多个组织提供能量，特别是为大脑、中枢神经系统、红细胞和工作肌肉提供能量。此外，充足的糖类供给有助于抑制蛋白质作为供能物质的分解。其次，糖类作为能量的一种储存形式存在于血液、肝脏和肌肉中，任何多余的糖类都会转化为脂肪。再次，糖类作为细胞膜成分参与介导细胞间的某些信号传导。最后，糖类也被认为是"脂肪引物"，因为脂肪的完全代谢需要糖类的参与。

Chapter 2   Lipids

第二章 脂 类

Lipids are a heterogeneous group of water-insoluble organic compounds, including oils, fats, waxes, and related compounds. Lipids are mainly composed of carbon, hydrogen and oxygen, and have a higher ratio of hydrogen and oxygen. Lipids can dissolve in ether, that is different from carbohydrates and proteins.

Lipids are the important energy source. When aerobic exercise intensity is lower than 60% to 65% $\dot{V}O_2max$ (Figure 2.1 A), or in the later stages of aerobic exercise lipids are the prominent source of energy (Figure 2.1 B). Therefore, it is necessary to have a better understanding of lipids biochemistry.

脂类(脂质)是一组不溶于水的有机分子,包括油、脂肪、蜡和相关化合物。脂类主要由碳、氢、氧元素组成,且氢、氧比例较高。与糖类和蛋白质不同的是,脂类可溶解于乙醚。

脂类是重要的供能物质。如图 2.1 所示,在运动强度低于 60%~65% 最大摄氧量（$\dot{V}O_2max$）的有氧运动中（图 2.1A）,以及长时间有氧运动的后期（图 2.1B）,脂类物质的供能作用更加突出。因此,有必要深入了解脂类物质的生物化学特征。

2.1 Classifications and Sources of Lipids
脂类的分类及来源

Lipids can be divided into three main groups: simple lipids, compound lipids, and derived lipids, including oils, fats, waxes, and related compounds (Figure 2.2). Most of the lipids in human body derive from dietary fat, and the overwhelming majority of them (90% to 95%) is in

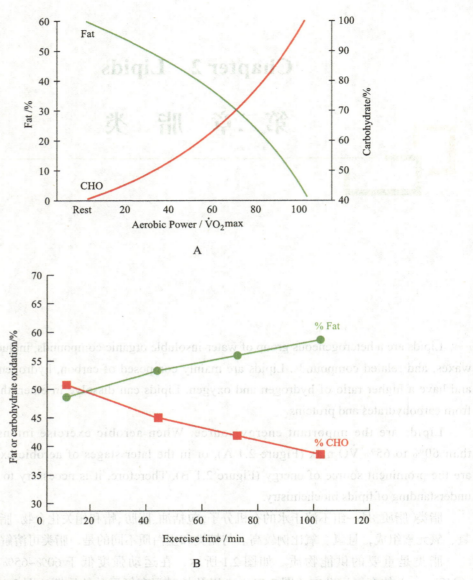

Figure 2.1　The use of carbohydrate and fat as energy surce during exercise

the form of triacylglycerols. The rest is mainly phospholipids. The free or esterified cholesterol is less than 0.5%.

　　脂类可分为简单脂、复合脂和衍生脂三大类，包括了油、脂肪、蜡等相关化合物（图2.2）。人体内的大部分脂质来自膳食脂肪，其中绝大多数（90%~95%）是以甘油三酯（三酰甘油）的形式存在的。剩余的主要是磷脂以及游离或酯化的胆固醇，这一部分在总脂质中占比不足 0.5%。

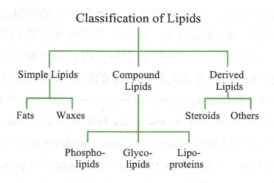

Figure 2.2　Classification of lipids

2.1.1 Triglycerides (Triacylglycerols)
甘油三酯（三酰甘油）

Triacylglycerols (TAGs), also known as fats, are the most abundant lipid category, consisting of a glycerol unit and three fatty acid units (Figure 2.3). Triacylglycerols must be broken down into fatty acids and glycerol before they can be used as energy source. In food, triacylglycerols are the main component of the fat and vegetable oils, accounting for 90% to 95% of the dietary fat.

甘油三酯，也就是我们通常所说的脂肪，是数量最多的一类脂质，由 1 个甘油和 3 个脂肪酸构成（图 2.3）。甘油三酯必须分解成脂肪酸和甘油后，才能作为供能物质被利用。在食物中，甘油三酯是脂肪和植物油的主要成分，占膳食脂肪的 90%~95%。

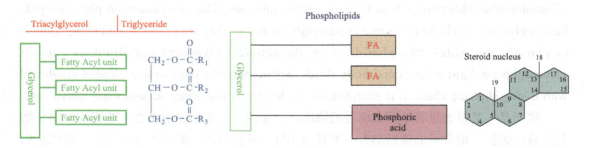

Figure 2.3　Structure of a triacylglycerol, phospholipid and steroid nucleus

Fatty acids, including unsaturated and saturated fatty acids, are the main usable energy form of lipids. Unsaturated fatty acids are subdivided into monounsaturated fatty acids and polyunsaturated fatty acids. Some polyunsaturated fatty acids, which are necessary as the precursors of other fatty acids, are unable to be synthesized in the body, and must be obtained from the diet, are classified as essential fatty acids. Other fatty acids that can be produced adequately in vivo are classified as nonessential fatty acids, such as saturated fatty acids.

脂肪酸，包括不饱和脂肪酸和饱和脂肪酸，是脂类的主要供能形式。不饱和脂肪酸又细分为单不饱和脂肪酸和多不饱和脂肪酸。有一些多不饱和脂肪酸作为其他脂肪酸的前体是人体必需的，但在体内无法合成，必须从食物中获得，因此被列为必需脂肪酸。其他包括饱和脂肪酸在内的能在体内合成并满足机体需求的脂肪酸被归类为非必需脂肪酸。

Saturated fatty acids are primarily found in animal products such as beef (52% saturated fatty acids), lamb, pork, chicken, egg yolk, and dairy fats of cream, milk, butter (62% saturated fatty acids), and cheese. Saturated fatty acids from plant products include coconut and palm oil, vegetable shortening, and hydrogenated margarine; commercially processed cakes, pies, and cookies contain plentiful amounts of these fatty acids. From a health perspective, individuals should consume no more than 10% of total daily energy intake of the saturated fatty acids (about 300 kcal). For example, the daily intake of saturated fatty acids of a young adult, whose average daily energy consumption is 3000 kcal, should be less than 30 to 35 g.

饱和脂肪酸主要存在于动物类食物中，如牛肉（含 52% 的饱和脂肪酸）、羊肉、猪肉、鸡肉、蛋黄等，此外在奶油、牛奶、黄油（含 62% 的饱和脂肪酸）和奶酪中也富含饱和脂肪酸。富含饱和脂肪酸的植物类食物包括椰子油、棕榈油、植物起酥油和人造黄油等。而蛋糕、派和饼干等市售的再加工食品也含有大量的饱、脂肪酸。从健康的角度来看，个人摄入的饱和脂肪酸不应超过每日摄入总能量的 10%（约 300 kcal），例如每日平均能耗在 3000 kcal 的青年男性，每日的饱和脂肪酸摄入量应低于 30~35 g。

2.1.2 Phospholipids
磷脂

Phospholipids are a category of lipids with remarkable structural diversity. The main function of amphipathic phospholipids is to form cell membranes. The most common phospholipids have a glycerol backbone (the same as triacylglycerols), so they are called glycerophospholipids or phosphoglycerides. Phosphatidic acid, the simplest glycerophospholipid, is a minor glycerophospholipid of cells and body fluids. Sphingomyelin is an amino alcohol combined with a long aliphatic chain. It is abundant in myelin sheath and wraps around many nerve cells.

磷脂是一类具有显著结构多样性的脂质，两亲性（亲水性和疏水性）磷脂的主要功能是形成细胞膜。最常见的磷脂都有一个甘油主链（就像甘油三酯的主链一样），所以它们又被称为甘油磷脂或磷酸甘油酯。磷脂酸是最简单的甘油磷脂，是细胞和体液中的一种较小的甘油磷脂。鞘磷脂是一种具有长脂肪链的氨基醇，富含于髓鞘中，包裹在许多神经细胞的周围。

2.1.3 Lipoprotein
脂蛋白

Lipoproteins are certain triglycerides and cholesterol surrounded by proteins and are mainly formed in the liver. Chylomicrons (CM), very low density lipoprotein (VLDL), low-density lipoprotein (LDL) and high-density lipoprotein (HDL) are the most common lipoproteins, and gradually decrease in size (Table 2.1). Chylomicron is the largest lipoprotein with the lowest density and highest lipid content, which is in charge of the transport of dietary triacylglycerols to extrahepatic tissues. The main responsibility of VLDL is to transport hepatic triacylglycerols to extrahepatic tissues. LDL is able to bind cholesterol and cholesterol esters and transports them to extrahepatic tissues. LDL, which binds cholesterol, tends to deposits in the blood vessel wall and becomes a risk factor for some diseases such as atherosclerosis. Thus, LDL is commonly known as "bad" cholesterol while HDL is often referred to as "good" cholesterol. HDL is the smallest lipoprotein with the highest density, lowest lipid and highest protein content. It is responsible for transporting cholesterol and cholesterol esters from extrahepatic tissues to the liver for further breakdown.

脂蛋白是一些被蛋白质包围的甘油三酯和胆固醇，主要在肝脏中形成。乳糜微粒（CM）、极低密度脂蛋白（VLDL）、低密度脂蛋白（LDL）和高密度脂蛋白（HDL）是最常见的体积递减的脂蛋白（表2.1）。其中，乳糜微粒的密度最低、脂质含量最高，负责将食物中的甘油三酯运输到肝外组织；极低密度脂蛋白的主要作用是将肝脏内的甘油三酯转运到肝外组织；低密度脂蛋白能结合胆固醇。由于结合了胆固醇的低密度脂蛋白容易沉积在血管壁，进而成为诱发动脉粥样硬化等疾病的危险因素，所以低密度脂蛋白通常被称为"坏胆固醇"。而高密度脂蛋白通常被称为"好胆固醇"，因为高密度脂蛋白是体积最小、密度最高、脂质含量最低、蛋白质含量最高的脂蛋白，它可以结合胆固醇和胆固醇酯，并将其从肝外组织运输到肝脏并被进一步分解。

Table 2.1　Composition of lipoproteins

Lipoprotein	Percentage composition					MWt $(\times 10^{6})$		
	Protein	Triacyl-glycerol	Cholesterol	Cholesterol ester	Phospho-lipid			
Chylomicrons	1–2	85–90	2–3	2–3	6–8	>400	More dense, moreprotein	More lipid
VLDL	8–10	50–55	6–8	14–16	16–20	5–10		
LDL	18–22	6–10	8–12	35–45	20–25	2–5		
HDL	47–52	3–6	2–4	12–18	25–30	0.2–0.4		

2.1.4 Steroids

类固醇

Steroids are another complex category of lipids, including bile salts, cholesterol and related compounds, as well as certain hormones (such as cortisone and the sex hormones).

Cholesterol is the most abundant steroid in the human body (about 240 g), and is crucial for synthesis of steroid hormones such as testosterone, progesterone, and estrogen. Cholesterol exists only in animal tissue and is widely found in the plasma membrane of all types of cells. The liver synthesizes about 70% of the body's cholesterol. A diet completely free of cholesterol can negatively affect the synthesis of sex hormones.

类固醇，另一种复杂的脂类，包括胆盐、胆固醇和相关化合物，以及某些激素（如可的松和性激素）。

胆固醇是人体中含量最丰富的类固醇（约为 240 g），它对合成睾酮、黄体酮和雌激素等类固醇激素至关重要。胆固醇只存在于动物组织中，并广泛分布在所有类型细胞的质膜中。肝脏合成人体约 70% 的胆固醇。完全缺乏胆固醇的饮食会对性激素的合成产生负面影响。

2.2 Digestion of Lipids
脂类的消化吸收

The digestion of dietary lipids begins in the stomach and is completed in the small intestine. In the small intestine, bile and pancreatic lipases break down TAGs into fatty acids and glycerol. When fatty acids diffuse through the intestinal wall, short and medium-chain fatty acids enter the blood directly. Since long-chain fatty acids are too large to pass into the blood, they are repackaged into chylomicrons. The chylomicrons enter the lymphatic system and then slowly enter the blood circulation. In the liver, muscle and fat tissue, chylomicrons are broken down into fatty acids and glycerol by lipoprotein lipase, which facilitates the passage of fatty acids and glycerol into the cells for storage or supply of energy. A small amount of fatty acids remain and circulate in the blood (Figure 2.4).

食物中脂类的消化是从胃开始，并在小肠中完成的。在小肠中，胆汁和胰脂肪酶将甘油三酯分解为脂肪酸和甘油。当脂肪酸在肠壁扩散时，短链和中链脂肪酸可以直接进入血液，长链脂肪酸因为太大而不能直接进入血液，所以长链脂肪酸被重新包装成乳糜微粒。乳糜微粒进入淋巴系统，然后缓慢地进入血液循环。在肝脏、肌肉和脂肪组织中，乳糜微粒被脂蛋白脂肪酶分解为脂肪酸和甘油，进而进入细胞被储存或提供能量。少量的脂肪酸残留在血液中并在血液中循环（图 2.4）。

2.3 Storage of Lipids
脂类的储存

In the human body, lipids can be found as TAGs in adipose tissue (about 80% of the adipose tissue mass consists of triacylglycerols), muscle, and blood. The adipose tissue that accumulates most of body fat is described as white adipose tissue, or white fat, and is mainly located under the skin (subcutaneous adipose tissue) and around internal organs (abdominal/visceral adipose tissue). Only about 50 g of brown adipose tissue exists in the upper chest and neck areas of adults.

In the muscle, more than 85% TAGs are stored in the form of lipid droplets between muscle

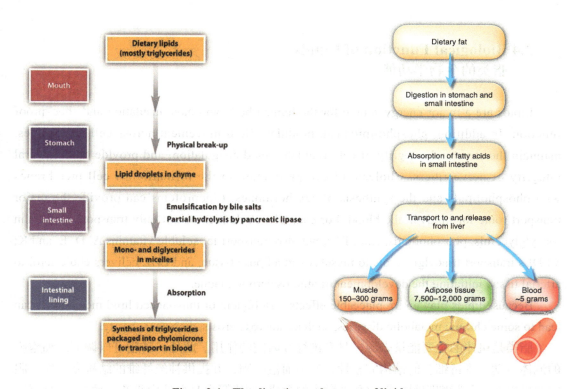

Figure2.4   The digestion and storage of lipid

fibers. The type I muscle fiber has much more TAGs than type II muscle fiber. The triglyceride content in the muscles of women is higher than that in men.

As the largest energy bank, a 75 kg man typically has 11 kg of fat or so, while a 62 kg woman has about 14 kg. Women generally have more fat than men by the percentage of body mass. Compared with non-athletes of the same gender, age, and body mass index, or BMI, athletes usually have lower body fat content.

在人体中，脂质以甘油三酯的形式存在于脂肪组织（约 80% 的脂肪组织由甘油三酯组成）、肌肉和血液中。聚集身体大部分脂肪的脂肪组织（称为白色脂肪组织或白色脂肪），主要位于皮肤下（皮下脂肪组织）和内脏周围（腹部 / 内脏脂肪组织）。在成年人的胸部上方和颈部有大约 50 g 的棕色脂肪组织。

在肌肉中，超过 85% 的甘油三酯都以脂滴的形式储存在肌纤维之间。I 型肌纤维中的甘油三酯含量高于 II 型纤维。女性的肌肉中的甘油三酯含量高于男性。

作为最大的能量库，通常体重为 75 kg 的男性体内会有约 11 kg 的脂肪，体重为 62 kg 的女性体内会有约 14 kg 的脂肪。一般来说，女性的脂肪占体重的百分比（体脂百分比）要比男性高。运动员的体脂含量通常低于同性别、同年龄、同体重指数（BMI）的非运动员。

2.4 Biological Function of Lipids
脂类的生物学功能

Lipids are a major energy source for the human body and have insulation and shockproof function. In addition, phospholipids can modulate fluid movement across cell membranes, maintain the structural integrity of cell, regulate blood coagulation, and provide the structural integrity of nerve fibers. Cholesterol can participate in the formation of cell membranes with phospholipids and the synthesis of sex hormones. Lipoproteins can provide the major transport route for lipids in the blood. For example, chylomicrons not only transport long-chain triacylglycerols, phospholipids, and FFAs, but also transport fat-soluble vitamins A, D, E, and K; VLDLs transport triacylglycerols to muscles and adipose tissue; and LDL delivers cholesterol to arterial tissue initiating the development of atherosclerotic plaque.

Because lipids play an irreplaceable effects, insufficient or unbalanced lipid metabolism can lead to some chronic metabolic diseases, such as atherosclerosis, diabetes, obesity.

脂类是机体的主要能量来源，具有绝缘和防震的作用。此外，磷脂可以调节跨细胞膜的流体运动、维持细胞的结构完整性、调节血液凝固，并提供神经纤维的结构完整性。胆固醇可以参与磷脂细胞膜的形成和性激素的合成，而脂蛋白是血液中脂类运输的主要途径，如乳糜微粒不仅可以运输长链甘油三酯、磷脂和脂肪酸，而且还可以运输脂溶性维生素 A、D、E 和 K；极低密度脂蛋白可以将甘油三酯转运到肌肉和脂肪组织；低密度脂蛋白可以将胆固醇输送到动脉组织，诱发动脉粥样硬化斑块的形成。

由于脂类具有某些不可替代的作用，脂类代谢的紊乱会成为诱发动脉粥样硬化、糖尿病、肥胖等慢性代谢性疾病的危险因素。

Chapter 3　Proteins

第三章　蛋白质

Proteins are the most abundant and functionally diverse molecules in the life system. All proteins contain carbon, hydrogen, oxygen and nitrogen atoms, and many also contain sulfur atoms. Nitrogen constitutes 16% of protein mass. Amino acids are the building blocks of proteins. Dozens or hundreds or even thousands of amino acids are joined in any possible sequence to assemble protein molecules. It is thought that there are 100,000 to 200,000 different proteins in the human body.

蛋白质是生物体中含量最丰富、功能最多样的分子。所有蛋白质都含有碳、氢、氧、氮等元素，此外，大多数蛋白质还含有硫原子。各种蛋白质的氮含量都接近16%。氨基酸是蛋白质的基本组成单位，数十个、数百个甚至数千个氨基酸以任何可能的顺序连接在一起，组成蛋白质分子。据推测，人体中可能有10万~20万种不同的蛋白质。

3.1 Classifications and Sources of Proteins
蛋白质的分类及来源

There are many ways to classify proteins. Based on the structure, proteins can be classified as fibrous proteins and globular proteins. Fibrous proteins, such as keratin, collagen, myosin, and elastin, are insoluble in water and usually serve as structural, connective, and protective functions. Globular proteins, such as serum albumin, hemoglobin and myoglobin, are soluble in aqueous media. Based on the function, proteins can be classified as catalytic proteins (enzymes), transport proteins, storage proteins, motor proteins, structural proteins, defensive proteins, messenger proteins, receptor proteins, and other regulatory proteins（Table 3.1）. In fact, many proteins have more than one function. For example, myosin is both a motor protein and an enzyme.

　　蛋白质的分类方法有很多种。根据蛋白质的结构特征，可以将蛋白质分为纤维蛋白和球状蛋白。在纤维蛋白中，角蛋白、胶原蛋白、肌球蛋白和弹性蛋白等都不溶于水，通常作为结构物质或者具有连接和保护功能。在球蛋白中，血清白蛋白、血红蛋白和肌红蛋白等则可溶于液态介质。如表 3.1 所示，根据蛋白质的功能差异，还可以将蛋白质分为催化蛋白（酶）、运输蛋白、储存蛋白、运动蛋白、结构蛋白、防御蛋白、信使蛋白、受体和其他调节蛋白。事实上，许多蛋白质有不止一种功能，例如，肌球蛋白既是一种运动蛋白，同时也是一种酶。

Table 3.1　Classification of Proteins by Biological Function

Catalytic Protein	Biological Function	Example
catalytic proteins	accelerate biological reactions	α-Amylase catalyzes the hydrolysis of starch and glycogen
transport proteins	transport substances from one place to another	Hemoglobin transports oxygen from the lungs throughout the body
storage proteins	provide storage of essential nutrients	Ferritin stores iron in the body
motor proteins	muscle contraction; cell division	Myosin is one protein needed for the contraction of muscles
structural proteins	provide strength and structure	Keratin is the primary protein of hair and wool
defensive proteins	protect cells or the organism from foreign substances	Immunoglobulins recognize and breakdown foreign molecules
messenger proteins	regulate the functioning of other proteins	Insulin regulates the activity of specific enzymes in the body
receptor proteins	molecular messengers	Insulin receptor bind with insulin to alter the biological activity of insulin
other regulatory proteins	control biological processes	The proteins control the flow of genetic information by binding to nucleic acids

There are 20 types of amino acids involved in the formation of proteins (Table 3.2), eight of these are described as essential amino acids because the body cannot make them and they must be obtained from the food we eat. The other 12 amino acids are often considered as non-essential amino acids, because the body can synthesize them from compounds already present in cells. Therefore proteins that contain all the essential amino acids in the quantity and good ratio for maintaining nitrogen balance, tissue growth and repair are referred to as complete proteins, while those lacking of one or more essential amino acids are referred to as incomplete proteins.

　　组成人体蛋白质的氨基酸有 20 种（表 3.2），其中 8 种氨基酸，由于身体不能合成，必须从食物中获得，而被称为必需氨基酸；剩下的 12 种氨基酸通常被认为是非必需氨基酸，因为人体可以利用细胞中已经存在的化合物来合成它们。因此，如果一种蛋白质含有的必需氨基酸数量和比例恰当，能够有利于维持氮平衡，并满足组织生长和修复的需求，那么这种蛋白质就被称为完全蛋白质。相反，如果某种蛋白质缺少一种或多种必需氨基酸，那么它就被称为不完全蛋白质。

Table3.2　Amino acid names and their abbreviations

Classification	Amino acid name	3-letter abbreviation	1-letter abbreviation
Non-essential	Alanine	Ala	A
	Arginine	Arg	R
	Asparagine	Asn	N
	Aspartate	Asp	D
	Cysteine	Cys	C
	Glutamate	Glu	E
	Glutamine	Gln	Q
	Glycine	Gly	G
	Histidine	His	H
	Proline	Pro	P
	Serine	Ser	S
	Tyrosine	Tyr	Y
Essential	Isoleucine	Ile	I
	Leucine	Leu	L
	Lysine	Lys	K
	Methionine	Met	M
	Phenylalanine	Phe	F
	Threonine	Thr	T
	Tryptophan	Trp	Y
	Valine	Val	V

3.2 Digestion of Proteins
蛋白质的消化吸收

Proteins are found in most foods of human diet. Good sources of proteins include all kinds of meat, dairy products, eggs, legumes, nuts, and cereals. Dietary proteins are first broken down into shorter peptides in the stomach, and then broken down into amino acids in the duodenum, under the concerted action of certain specific enzymes (Figure 3.1). The amino acids that enter the circulation are firstly absorbed and maintained by the liver, and then absorbed by extrahepatic tissues. Humans typically ingest about 10% to 15% of their total calories from protein.

The amino acid sequence of dietary proteins differs from that of humans. After the digestion and absorption, amino acids will be recombined according to the needs of the human body. All tissues are nourished by dietary amino acids. Furthermore, branched-chain amino acids (leucine, isoleucine, valine), glutamine, and aspartate can enter the energy pathways through deamination to regenerate energy.

　　食物中的蛋白质种类及数量非常丰富，各种肉类、乳制品、鸡蛋、豆类、坚果和谷类等都是较好的蛋白质来源。食物中的蛋白质首先在胃中分解为较短的肽，然后在某些特定酶的协同作用下在十二指肠分解为氨基酸（图 3.1）。进入循环的氨基酸首先被肝脏吸收和储存，然后被肝外组织吸收。人体所需总热量的 10%~15% 来自蛋白质。

　　食物蛋白的氨基酸序列与人类蛋白质序列不同，因此，消化吸收后的氨基酸会根据人体的需要重新组合。所有组织所需要的氨基酸都来自于食物。此外，支链氨基酸（亮氨酸、异亮氨酸、缬氨酸）、谷氨酰胺和天门冬氨酸可以通过脱氨基参与能量代谢，并生成能量。

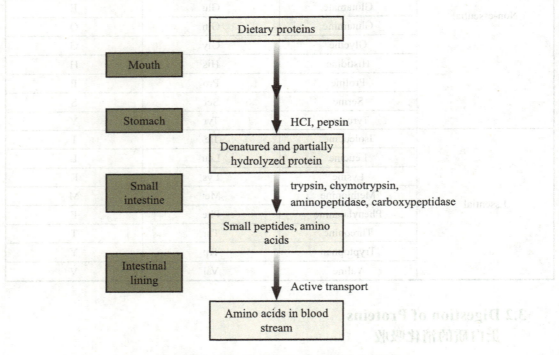

Figure3.1　The digestion and storage of protein

3.3 Storage of Proteins
蛋白质的储存

Protein makes up 12% to 15% of the body mass. Skeletal muscles contain the largest quantity of protein, about 6 to 8 kg, which accounted for 60% to 70% in total. Whether proteins come from food or are synthesised by the body itself, 99% of them are in the form of living tissues, such as muscle, visceral tissues and blood plasma. The remaining 1% (approximately 170 to 200 g) exists in cells as a pool of free amino acids and used primarily for the repair and maintenance of cells and tissues. Amino acids, which are not used to synthesize protein or other compounds, or not available for energy metabolism, provide substrates for gluconeogenesis, or are converted to triacylglycerol for storage in adipocytes. Therefore, there are limited amino acid reserves in the body.

蛋白质占人体重量的 12%~15%，其中骨骼肌所含蛋白质最多，为 6~8 kg，占蛋白质总量的 60%~75%。无论是来自食物的蛋白质还是体内自身合成的蛋白质，其中 99% 都是以活体组织的形式存在，例如肌肉、内脏组织和血浆。剩下的 1%（170~200 g）则作为游离氨基酸池存在于细胞中，主要用于细胞和组织的修复和维护。不能用于合成蛋白质及其他化合物或不能用于能量代谢的氨基酸，可以为糖异生提供底物或转化为甘油三酯储存在脂肪细胞中。所以，体内的氨基酸储备很少。

3.4 Biological Function of Proteins
蛋白质的生物学功能

Almost every life process depends on proteins, so proteins can participate in any biochemical process, and have a wide range of functions. Unlike fats and carbohydrates that can be stored in cells, once proteins enter the body, they will be used in different areas of the body to synthesize/maintain tissues and functional compounds (e.g., muscles, hormones, and enzymes), provide components needed to make nonprotein compounds (e.g., some neurotransmitters), transport fats and oxygen (e.g., hemoglobin, albumin), act as buffers to maintain blood pH, or become a substrate for production of glucose (gluconeogenesis) and generate energy.

几乎每个生命过程都依赖于蛋白质，所以蛋白质可以参与任何生物化学反应过程，并发挥多种生物学功能。蛋白质并不像脂肪和糖类那样可以存储在细胞里，所以蛋白质一旦进入机体后，就会在不同部位参与组成结构物质或功能物质（如肌肉、激素、酶等）而发挥作用，为非蛋白化合物（如一些神经递质）的合成提供原料，运输脂肪和氧气（如血红蛋白、白蛋白），作为缓冲物质维持血液 pH 值，或者成为葡萄糖生成（糖异生）和能量生成的底物。

Chapter 4　Vitamins

第四章　维生素

Vitamins, which have no common chemical structure features, are a diverse group of organic compounds required by the human body in minute amounts. Vitamins serve as regulators of numerous metabolic processes in the body, although they provide neither energy nor raw materials for tissue building.

维生素是一类人体必需的微量有机化合物，它们没有共同的特殊化学结构特征。维生素虽然既不提供能量，也不提供构成组织所需要的原料，但它在人体的多种代谢过程中起着重要的调节作用。

4.1 Classifications and Sources of Vitamins
维生素的分类及来源

Vitamins are present in food in minuscule amounts. Based on their solubility in water, 13 vitamins are classified as water-soluble vitamins and fat-soluble vitamins (Table 4.1). Water-soluble vitamins are widely found in food, including Vitamin C (ascorbate) and B-complex vitamins. Fat-soluble vitamins are found in dietary fat, including Vitamin A, D, E, and K.

食物中的维生素含量较低。根据维生素在水中的溶解性，13 种维生素可以被分为水溶性维生素和脂溶性维生素（表 4.1）。水溶性维生素广泛存在于食物中，包括维生素 C（抗坏血酸）和复合 B 族维生素；脂溶性维生素存在于食物脂肪中，包括维生素 A、D、E、K。

Table 4.1　The classification of vitamins

Classification			Sources	Function
Water-soluble vitamin		Vitamin C (or Ascorbate)	Peppers, broccoli, citrus fruits, green leaves, potatoes, and tomatoes	A reducing agent (or antioxidant) for several enzymes; be needed for the synthesis of norepinephrine
	B-complex vitamins	Vitamin B$_1$ (or Thiamine)	Legumes, whole-grain cereals, pork, and liver	Be converted into thiamine pyrophosphate, participating in the cleavage of bonds lying next to carbonyl groups
		Vitamin B$_2$ (or Riboflavin)	Liver, meat, eggs, milk, other dairy products, legumes, and dark-green vegetables	Precursor of FAD and FMN
		Niacin	Organ meats, red meat, poultry, fish, nuts, whole-grain cereals, and legumes	Precursor of NAD and NADP
		Vitamin B$_6$ (or Pyridoxine)	Organ meats, red meat, poultry, fish, egg yolk, pistachios, whole-grain cereals, legumes, bananas, and potatoes	Be converted into pyridoxal phosphate, a coenzyme specializing in the transfer of amino groups among compounds
		Vitamin B$_{12}$ (or Cobalamin)	Animal-based foods: clams, liver, meat, fish, milk, other dairy products, and egg yolk	–
		Folate	Dark-green leafy vegetables, yeast, beans, liver, nuts, whole grains, and some fruits	
		Pantothenate	Liver, red meat, poultry, fish, milk, other dairy products, egg yolk, legumes, and whole grains	A part of the structure of coenzyme A
		Biotin	Liver, red meat, fish, poultry, eggs, cheese, nuts, and some vegetables	A coenzyme for enzymes involved in biosynthesis of glucose and fatty acid, as well as degradation of some amino acids
Fat-soluble vitamin		Vitamin A (or Retinol)	Liver, butter, cheese, fortified milk, egg yolk, and fish liver oil; carrots, dark-green leafy vegetables, and oranges	Be necessary for vision and for the development and maintenance of several tissues
		Vitamin D (or Cholecalciferol)	Mushrooms, milk, margarine, cereals, egg yolk, and oily fish	Be crucial for bone health, development of the skin, and muscle function and performance
		Vitamin E (or α-tocopherol)	Vegetable oils, nuts, whole-grain products, egg yolk, and darkgreen leafy vegetables	An antioxidant protecting against oxidation and damage by radicals

Classification		Sources	Function
Fat-soluble vitamin	Vitamin K (or Phylloquinone)	Green vegetables and vegetable oils	Be required in the production of the mature and functional form of proteins that mediate blood coagulation or regulate bone metabolism

(FAD: flavin adenine dinucleotide; FMN: flavin mononucleotide; NAD: Nicotinamide Adenine Dinucleotide; NADP: Nicotinamide Adenine Dinuleotide Phosphate)

With the exception of vitamin D, vitamins cannot be produced in the human body, because we lack the enzymes that catalyze certain biosynthetic reactions. Thus, vitamins must be supplied through diet or supplements. Vitamins can repeatedly participate in metabolic reactions without being consumed, so a well-balanced diet can provide adequate amounts of all vitamins, regardless of the age and physical activity level.

除了维生素 D 之外，因为机体缺乏酶来催化某些生物合成反应，人体不能合成其他维生素，所以必须通过饮食或补充剂来补充维生素。维生素可以反复参与代谢反应且不会被消耗，因此，无论年龄和身体活动水平如何，人们只要保持均衡的饮食，都能确保摄取到全面且足量的维生素。

4.2 Digestion of Vitamins
维生素的消化吸收

After being ingested from food, the water-soluble vitamins are digested with body fluids, and the fat-soluble vitamins are released, absorbed, and transported with dietary lipids and then enter the liver for dispersion to various tissues.

进食后，水溶性维生素将伴随体液的消化而被吸收，而脂溶性维生素则与食物中的脂类一起被释放、吸收，并转运到肝脏，进而分散到全身各种组织。

4.3 Storage of Vitamins
维生素的储存

Water-soluble vitamins are dispersed in body fluids and readily excreted in urine without excessive storage. Fat-soluble vitamins dissolve and remain in the body's fatty tissues, so excessive intake of fat-soluble vitamins is more likely to induce the toxic reactions than water-soluble vitamins.

Vitamin A is present in food in two distinct forms: retinol and carotenoids. Retinol can be found, in large amount, in animal-based foods such as liver, butter, cheese, fortified milk, egg yolk, and fish liver oil. Carotenoids, represented by β-carotene, are abundant in plant foods, such as carrots (the color to which is related to β-carotene), dark-green leafy vegetables, and oranges (Table 4.1). Vitamin D has two main forms: ergocalciferol, or vitamin D_2, and cholecalciferol, or vitamin D_3. Ergocalciferol is found naturally in mushrooms; it is also added to milk, margarine, and breakfast cereals. Cholecalciferol, on the other hand, is present in egg yolks and oily fish (such as salmon, mackerel, and sardines) (Table 4.1). However, food normally only provides about one-tenth of our required vitamin D. The remaining nine-tenths are synthesized as cholecalciferol in our body, after being exposed to sunlight. Therefore, vitamin D is one of the few vitamins that we can synthesize, and it is also the unique vitamin that synthesis is greater than the intake. In the human body, the liver stores vitamins A and D, while vitamin E is distributed throughout the body's fatty tissues. Vitamin K is stored only in small amounts, mainly in the liver.

水溶性维生素分散在体液中，容易随尿液排出体外，因此不会过量储存。脂溶性维生素溶解在脂肪组织中，容易滞留，因此摄入过量的脂溶性维生素比水溶性维生素更容易引起中毒反应。

维生素 A 以两种不同的形式存在于食物中：视黄醇和类胡萝卜素。大量的视黄醇可以在动物性食品中发现，如肝脏、黄油、奶酪、强化牛奶、蛋黄和鱼肝油；类胡萝卜素，以 β-胡萝卜素为代表，在植物性食物中大量存在，如胡萝卜（其颜色来源于 β-胡萝卜素）、深绿色叶蔬菜和橙子（表 4.1）。维生素 D 有两种主要形式：麦角钙化醇（或维生素 D_2）和胆钙化醇（或维生素 D_3）。蘑菇中富含天然的麦角钙化醇，麦角钙化醇还被添加到牛奶、人造黄油和早餐麦片中；蛋黄和富含脂肪酸的鱼类（如鲑鱼、鲭鱼和沙丁鱼）中含有胆钙化醇（表4.1）。然而，食物提供的维生素 D 通常只占人体所需量的 1/10，剩下的 9/10 是通过我们晒太阳后在体内合成的胆钙化醇。因此，维生素 D 是少数几种我们能合成的维生素之一，也是唯一一种我们合成的比吃的多的维生素。在人体内，肝脏储存维生素 A 和 D，而维生素 E 分布在全身的脂肪组织中。维生素 K 只能少量储存，主要在肝脏中。

4.4 Biological Function of Vitamins
维生素的生物学功能

Various vitamins play a variety of irreplaceable biological functions in the body (Figure 4.1). For example, Vitamin C deficiency causes scurvy, which involves decomposition of connective tissue in blood vessels, skin, gums, tendons, and cartilage. Prolonged Vitamin B_1 deficiency results in beriberi, a disease that manifests as damage to the nervous system and heart, which may ultimately lead to death. Vitamin B_2 deficiency causes cracks at the corners of the mouth, glossitis (tongue lesions), and dermatitis (skin lesions). Chronic niacin deficiency leads to pellagra, which is characterized by severe dermatitis, diarrhea, and dementia. Symptoms of Vitamin B_6 deficiency include skin diseases, weakness, depression, confusion, and anemia due to impaired heme biosynthesis. Vitamin A deficiency can cause nyctalopia, or night blindness. Vitamin D deficiency can cause rickets in children and osteomalacia in adults. And Vitamin K deficiency can cause hemorrhage.

Vitamins do not supply energy, but they act as essential links and regulators in the energy metabolism. For example, water-soluble vitamins largely act as coenzymes and play many important roles in regulating energy production in the catabolism of carbohydrates, fats, and proteins.

各种维生素在机体中发挥着多种不可替代的生物学功能（图 4.1）。例如，维生素 C 缺乏会导致坏血病，坏血病涉及血管、皮肤、牙龈、肌腱和软骨中的结缔组织分解；长期缺乏维生素 B_1 会导致脚气病，这种疾病表现为神经系统损伤和心脏损伤，最终可能导致死亡；维生素 B_2 缺乏会导致嘴角开裂、舌炎（舌头病变）和皮炎（皮肤病变）；长期缺乏烟酸会导致糙皮病，其特征是严重的皮炎、腹泻和痴呆；维生素 B_6 缺乏的症状包括皮肤紊乱、虚弱、抑郁、精神混乱，以及血红素生物合成受损导致的贫血；缺乏维生素 A 会导致夜盲症；缺乏维生素 D 会导致儿童佝偻病和成人骨软化症；缺乏维生素 K 会导致出血。

虽然维生素不提供能量，但是它们在释放能量反应中起着重要的信号传导和调节作用。例如，水溶性维生素主要作为辅酶，在调节糖类、脂肪和蛋白质分解代谢过程中的产能反应中发挥重要作用。

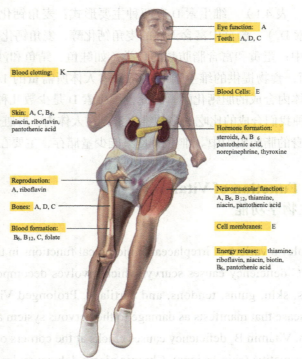

Figure 4.1 Biologic functions of vitamins

Chapter 5　Minerals

第五章　矿物质

There are mainly 22 kinds of metal elements participating in body composition, collectively known minerals, accounting for about 4% of the human body mass. Minerals do not provide energy, but they are considered to be essential in the human body. Because minerals combine with other chemical substances or exist alone, they are used as components of enzymes, hormones, and vitamins to regulate numerous body functions and tissues building.

　　参与人体组成的金属元素主要有 22 种，统称为矿物质，约占人体质量的 4%。矿物质虽不能提供能量，但它们是人体所必需的，因为矿物质与其他化学物质结合或单独存在，它们被用作酶、激素和维生素的成分来调节人体的许多功能和组织的形成。

5.1 Classifications and Sources of Minerals
矿物质的分类及来源

Based on chemical properties, minerals are divided into metallic and non-metallic minerals (Table 5.1). Metallic minerals in the diet include sodium, potassium, calcium, magnesium, iron, copper, zinc, chromium, manganese, and molybdenum. Non-metallic minerals in the diet include chlorine, phosphorus, selenium, fluorine, and iodine. Based on the needs of the human body, there are major minerals (daily requirement >100 mg) and minor or trace minerals (daily requirement <100 mg).

　　矿物质按其化学性质可以分为金属和非金属两类。食物中的金属矿物质包括钠、钾、钙、镁、铁、铜、锌、铬、锰、钼等；非金属矿物质包括氯、磷、硒、氟、碘等（表 5.1）。根据人体的需要量，矿物质又可以分为常量矿物质（每日需要量大于 100 mg）和微量矿物质（每日需要量小于 100 mg）。

Table 5.1　Classification and food source of minerals

Classification		Food Source	Function
Metal minerals	Sodium (Na)	Salt	Maintain the water content, blood pressure, electrical transmission of nerve signals, and muscle activity
Metal minerals	Potassium (K)	Potatoes, bananas, citrus fruits, several vegetables, liver, red meat, poultry, fish, milk, and other dairy products	Maintain the balance of fluids and to allow the electrical excitation of nerve and muscle cells
	Calcium (Ca)	Dairy products, sardines, dark-green leafy vegetables, legumes, and nuts	Regulates a multitude of biological processes, such as neural transmission, muscle activity, glycogen breakdown, and gene expression
	Magnesiu (Mg)	Nuts, legumes, whole-grain products, dark-green leafy vegetables, and seafood	A cofactor for about two hundred characterized enzymes
	Iron (Fe)	Liver, red meat, poultry, seafood, legumes, nuts, and dark-green leafy vegetables	Be essential for the uptake, transport, storage, and utilization of O_2 for ATP production
	Copper (Cu)	Liver, shellfish, legumes, nuts, seeds, potatoes, and whole-grain products	A cofactor for cytochrome c oxidase
	Zinc (Zn)	Oysters, liver, red meat, poultry, cheese, egg yolk, legumes, nuts, and whole-grain products	Be necessary for growth, immunity, and appetite
	Chromium (Cr)	Broccoli, processed meat, whole-grain products, nuts, potatoes, and certain fruits (for example, grapes)	Uncertain
	Manganese (Mn)	Whole-grain products, beans, nuts, leafy vegetables, and teas	A cofactor of some metabolism regulation and antioxidant protection enzymes
	Molybdenum (Mo)	Liver, whole-grain products, legumes, and nuts	A cofactor involved in the oxidation of some amino acids and purines
Nonmetal minerals	Chlorine (Cl)	Almost all foods	Maintain the fluid balance and electrical charges balance of across cell membranes, produce hydrochloric acid
	Phosphorus (P)	Liver, red meat, poultry, seafood, egg yolk, dairy products, nuts, legumes, and grain products	Be present as phosphate to conjunct with Ca^{2+} and some organic biological compounds
	Selenium (Se)	Brazil nuts, organ meats, seafood, red meat, and poultry	Part of some antioxidant enzymes
	Fluorine (F)	Fluoridated drinking water, tea and seafood	Be incorporated into bones and teeth
	Iodine (I)	Iodized salt, seafood, dairy products, potatoes, grains, poultry, and eggs	Part of the structure of two thyroid hormones, triiodothyronine and thyroxine

5.2 Biological Function of Minerals
矿物质的生物学功能

There is a consensus that metals are essential to the human body. Metals serve a variety of functions, such as maintaining the body's water content, transmitting nerve signals, forming bones and teeth, serving as cofactors of enzymes, and regulating gene expression. Non-metals are involved in fluid balance, digestion, bone and tooth formation, antioxidant defense, growth, and development. Mineral deficiency may cause neurological, muscular, and cardiac problems, as well as weak bones, anemia, and impaired growth and development.

A short-term sodium deficiency may appear during prolonged exercise as hyponatremia, which causes nausea, vomiting, headache, fatigue, and muscle cramps. Potassium deficiency, which is rare, causes muscle weakness and cardiac arrhythmia. The deficiency of calcium causes rickets in children and osteoporosis in adults. The deficiency of magnesium causes muscle weakness, muscle tremor, muscle cramps, and cardiac arrhythmia. Iron deficiency may lead to reduced synthesis of hemoglobin, myoglobin, and proteins of the electron-transport chain. Chronic iron deficiency will cause iron deficiency anemia. Zinc deficiency depresses growth, immunity, and appetite. Effects of copper, chromium and molybdenum deficiency have not been observed yet.

Some minor minerals, such as boron (B), silicon (Si), vanadium (V), nickel (Ni), and arsenic (As), have been proposed as components of the human body. However, their biological functions are unknown. Therefore, it is possible that their presence in the body may simply be the result of consuming foods that contain them.

矿物质在人体中是必不可少的。金属矿物质有多种功能，如维持体内水分含量、传递神经信号、形成骨骼和牙齿、充当酶的辅因子及调节基因表达；非金属矿物质参与体液平衡、消化、骨骼和牙齿的形成、抗氧化防御、生长和发育。缺乏矿物质可能导致神经、肌肉和心脏问题，以及骨质疏松、贫血和生长发育障碍。

在长时间运动中可能会出现短暂的钠缺乏，表现为低钠血症，可引起恶心、呕吐、头痛、疲劳和肌肉痉挛；钾缺乏是较为罕见的，但一旦发生会导致肌肉无力和心律失常；钙缺乏往往与儿童佝偻病和成人骨质疏松症密切相关；镁缺乏则会导致肌肉无力、肌肉震颤、肌肉痉挛和心律失常；铁缺乏可能导致血红蛋白、肌红蛋白和电子传递链蛋白的合成减少，长期缺铁还会引起缺铁性贫血；缺锌会抑制生长、免疫力和食欲。目前没有观察到铜、铬和钼等缺乏带来的不良影响。

一些微量矿物质，如硼（B）、硅（Si）、钒（V）、镍（Ni）和砷（As），虽然已被证实是人体的组成部分，但是它们的生物学功能还不清楚。因此，这些矿物质在体内的存在可能仅仅是人们食用了含有这些矿物质的食物的结果。

Chapter 6　Water

第六章　水

Water constitutes 45% to 75% of total body mass, depending on age, gender, and the amount of adipose tissue (fat) in the body. Typically, water accounts for 75% of muscle weight, 80% of brain, 83% of blood, 90% of lungs, 64% of skin, 30% of bones and less than 20% of the fat mass. Water carries essential nutrients to each cell and carries away the end products of its metabolism, so the body's demand for water far exceeds the demands for any other nutrient.

受到年龄、性别和体脂含量等因素的影响，水占人体总质量的45%~75%。一般情况下，水占肌肉重量的75%，大脑重量的80%，血液重量的83%，肺重量的90%，皮肤重量的64%，骨骼重量的30%和脂肪重量的不到20%。水为每一个细胞输送必需的营养素并带走其代谢的最终产物，因此，机体对水的需要远远超过对其他任何营养成分的需求。

6.1 Water Balance
水平衡

Under normal circumstances, the human body does not store excess water, and any excess water is no longer stored, and the volume of body fluids remains dynamically balanced. The body can obtain water through ingestion (2300 mL/d) and metabolic synthesis (200 mL/d), a total of about 2500 mL/d. Water loss mainly occurs in four ways: the kidneys excrete about 1500 mL/d through urine, the skin evaporates about 600 mL/d, the lungs exhale about 300 mL/d in the form of water vapor, and the gastrointestinal tract eliminates about 100 mL/d in feces (Figure 6.1). The body's water intake and output are regulated through a delicate balance mechanism to maintain the body's water balance. More water intake leads to more excretion and less intake of water results in less excretion in health condition.

About two-thirds of total body fluid is intracellular fluid, and the rest, called extracellular fluid, includes all other body fluids. 80% of the extracellular fluid is interstitial fluid, and the other 20% is blood plasma, which is the liquid portion of blood (Figure 6.2). Water can enter and exit freely through the cell membrane, so cells cannot directly regulate the water content by controlling water entering and leaving the cell.

正常情况下，人体不储存多余的水分，人体内的水分（体液）保持动态平衡。人体可以通过食物、饮料（2300 mL/d）和代谢合成（200 mL/d）获得水分，总共约2500 mL/d。人体丢失水分主要以四种方式发生：肾脏排出约1500 mL/d的尿液、皮肤蒸发约600 mL/d的汗液、肺排出约300 mL/d的水蒸气，以及胃肠道排出约100 mL/d的粪便（图6.1）。机体对水的摄取和排出都会受到一种精密平衡机制的调节，以保持体内的水分平衡，多摄取则多排出，少饮水则少排出。

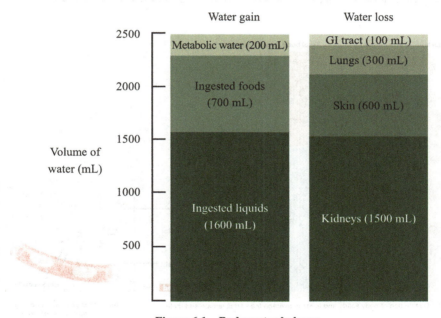

Figure 6.1   Body water balance

在人体的体液中，大约2/3是细胞内液体，另外的1/3为细胞外液体，包括细胞外的所有其他体液。细胞外液的80%为组织间液，其余20%为血浆，即血液的液体部分（图6.2）。水能够自由地进出细胞膜，因此细胞并不能直接通过将水吸入或排出来调节细胞内水分含量。

Exercise in hot weather will increase the body's water requirement by five or six times above normal requirements. During prolonged exercise, excessive sweating and consuming large volumes of water will cause hyponatremia or water intoxication. The first appearing symptom of dehydration is thirst (Table 6.1), by which time the body has lost approximately 500 mL of fluids. When the body loses about 5% of its body weight, symptoms such as headache, fatigue, forgetfulness and rapid heart rate will appear. At this time, the body will use most of the water in the body, including the water originally in sweat, to maintain blood pressure and life. When the body loses about 7% of its water, shock is most likely to occur. If too much water is lost and not replenished in time, it can be life-threatening. Therefore, people should drink ehough water regularly every day, rather than drink until thirsty.

在炎热的天气里锻炼会增加身体对水分的需求，比正常情况高出 5~6 倍。在长时间的运动中，过多地出汗或摄取大量的水会引起低钠血症或水中毒。脱水的第一个症状就是口渴（表6.1），此时人体已失去约 500 mL 体液。当机体失水 5% 左右会明显出现头痛、疲惫、健忘和心跳加速等症状，这时机体将动用体内绝大多数水分，包括原本在汗液中的那些水分，来保持血压以维持生命；失水 7% 左右时很可能发生休克。如果失水过多而又得不到补充，会危及生命。因此，人们应该每天定时补充一定的水分，而不是等到口渴才去喝水。

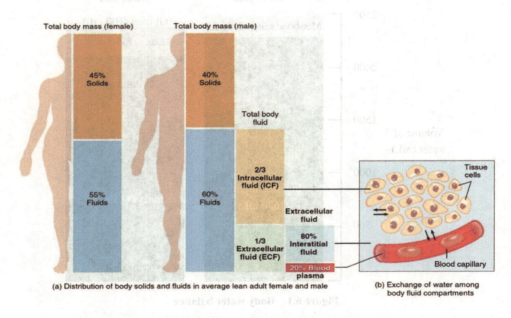

(a) Distribution of body solids and fluids in average lean adult female and male

(b) Exchange of water among body fluid compartments

Figure 6.2   The distribution of body water

Table 6.1　Symptoms of mild dehydration and severe dehydration

Mild dehydration (Water loss is less than 5% of body weight)	Severe dehydration (Water loss is greater than 5% of body weight)
Thirst	Pale skin
Weight loss	Blue lips and fingertips
Dry skin	Dizziness, directional force disappeared
Dry mouth, throat and body surface	Shortness and lightening of breath
Pulse quickened	The pulse becomes faster, weaker, and irregular
Lower blood pressure	Blood to thicken
Weakness	Shock, epilepsy
Renal failure	Coma, death
Decreased urine volume, Urine thicken	

6.2 Function of Water in the Body
水的生物学功能

Water is a ubiquitous nutrient. Firstly, as the cell composition, water provides the basic conditions for the chemical reactions of metabolism and participates in it. Secondly, water acts as a transport medium for nutrients and metabolic wastes in the body, which can not only transport nutrients to all parts of the body but also remove metabolic wastes from the body. Moreover, water provides shock protection for sensitive tissues such as the spinal cord, and the aqueous fluid in the eye maintains normal pressure on the retina and lens. Water is also a lubricant in the digestive tract and all mucus tissues. Another property of water is its thermal regulation. The skin removes excess heat from the body by secreting sweat to evaporate water. In hot and humid weather, the sweat doesn't evaporate because there's so much water in the surrounding air, so the body temperature tends to rise.

水是一种无处不在的营养素。首先，作为细胞的组成成分，水为新陈代谢的化学反应提供了基本的条件，并参与其中。其次，作为体内营养物质和代谢废物的运输介质，水可以在为全身各处输送营养物质的同时，清除体内的代谢废物。水可以在关节中起着润滑和缓冲的作用。同样，水还为那些比较敏感的组织如脊髓提供防震保护，眼睛内的房水能保持视网膜和晶状体的正常压力。水还是消化管道和所有黏液组织中的润滑剂。水还有一个特性就是它的热调节能力。皮肤通过分泌汗液蒸发水分带走体内多余的热量，在湿热的天气中，由于周围的空气中含水量大，汗液不能蒸发，体温容易升高。

○ Summary

Carbohydrates, lipids, proteins, vitamins, minerals, and water have characteristic functions for health and exercise performance. An optimal dietary supply requires adequate amounts of those to maintain tissue repair and growth, without excess energy intake at the same time. People who exercise regularly, must obtain sufficient energy and macronutrients to replenish liver and muscle glycogen, provide amino acid building blocks for tissue growth and repair, and maintain adequate lipid intake to provide essential fatty acids and fat-soluble vitamins through regular intake of a nutritionally well-balanced diet.

○ 本篇小结

糖类、脂类、蛋白质、维生素、矿物质和水对健康和运动都有其独特的作用。理想的饮食应给机体提供足够的营养物质来维持组织修复和生长的需要，而不提供过多的能量。有运动习惯的人，必须通过规律的均衡饮食获得足够的糖、脂、蛋白质，在满足机体能量需求的同时，提供充足的肝糖原、肌糖原储备，为组织生长和修复提供氨基酸原料，提供必要的脂肪酸和脂溶性维生素。

Part II　Exercise Metabolism
第二篇　运动代谢

○ Learning Objectives

- Distinguish exercise parameters: type, intensity, duration, and frequency.
- Distinguish between ATP–ADP cycle and energy resynthesis systems.
- Outline the metabolic characteristics of carbohydrates, lipids and proteins in exercise.
- Outline the integration of metabolic regulation in exercise.
- Distinguish the adaptation of different training.

○ 学习目标

- 掌握运动参数：运动类型、运动强度、持续时间和运动频率。
- 掌握 ATP–ADP 循环及能量再合成系统。
- 了解运动中糖类、脂类和蛋白质的代谢特征。
- 掌握运动中代谢调节的整合作用。
- 了解不同运动引起的代谢适应性变化。

Living organisms are in a state of constantly exchanging substances and energy with the environment, and thousands of chemical reactions have taken place to support all the essential processes of the body, which is called metabolism. Catabolism and anabolism are two chemical reactions that exchange substances and energy. The chemical reactions that mainly provides energy to muscles to exercise are called exercise metabolism. The change of exercise metabolism rate depends on exercise parameters, individual characteristics in exercising, and environmental factors. Through some metabolic control (such as allosteric regulation, covalent modification, change of substrate concentration, change of enzyme concentration, and nerve and hormonal control), regular exercise elicits many metabolic changes to increase performance and improve health or prevent disease. These effects are called exercise adaptation or training adaptation, and usually last from several days to several months after the exercise training.

生物体处于一种与环境不断进行物质和能量交换的状态，这种由成千上万个化学反应来维持的状态就是新陈代谢。分解代谢和合成代谢是物质和能量交换的两类化学反应，以骨骼肌提供运动所需能量为主的化学反应称为运动代谢。运动代谢率的变化取决于运动要素、运动个体特征和环境因素。有规律的运动可以通过一些代谢控制（如变构调节、共价修饰、改变底物浓度、改变酶浓度及神经和激素调控）引起许多代谢适应性变化以提高运动表现，改善健康或保护身体免受疾病的侵袭。这些效果称为运动适应或训练适应，通常在停止运动后仍可持续几天到几个月。

Chapter 7　Exercise Parameters

第七章　运动参数

Physical activity is defined as any body movement produced by muscle activity that results in energy expenditure above the resting level. Based on physical activity, exercise is defined as planned and organized body movement. The exercise training (repeated exercise) will result in learning and improving one or more physical skills, or maintaining and improving one or more physical abilities.

Exercise does not exert the same effects on metabolism. It is necessary to understand exercise parameters to clarify which types of metabolic changes we are talking about. Exercise type, intensity, duration, and frequency are the four main parameters of exercise.

体力活动是指由骨骼肌收缩引起的能量消耗高于基础代谢水平的身体活动。在体力活动的基础上，运动被定义为有计划、有组织的身体运动。通过运动训练（反复练习）可以使人学会和提高一项或多项身体技能，或维持和提高一项或多项身体能力。

运动对新陈代谢的作用不尽相同，有必要了解运动相关要素，以便于阐明我们所讨论的代谢变化适用于哪些类型。运动类型、运动强度、持续时间和运动频率是运动的四个主要参数。

7.1 Exercise Type
运动类型

Endurance exercise, resistance exercise and sprint exercise are the three most common types of exercise. Endurance exercise is characterized by prolonged periods and low-resistance muscle activity. This activity can be continuous or intermittent. For example, jogging is a continuous endurance exercise, and biathlon is an intermittent (or interval) endurance exercise. Resistance exercise involves short-term muscle activity that counteracts high-resistance. Weightlifting is one of the typical resistance exercises. Sprint exercise consists of short periods of maximum muscle activity against low-resistance, such as 50 meters competitive swimming.

According to the predominant ways of energy production during exercise, there is another way to describe exercise as being aerobic exercise and anaerobic exercise. Aerobic exercise mainly obtains energy from metabolic processes that directly or indirectly require oxygen. Anaerobic exercise mainly draws energy from processes that do not require oxygen. Endurance exercise is often described as aerobic exercise, while resistance and sprint exercises are usually anaerobic exercise.

Any type of exercise relies on a mixture of aerobic and anaerobic metabolic processes in the proportion. But we always ignore the word "mainly", leading people to believe that an exercise can be completely aerobic or completely anaerobic. Therefore, when we describe exercise or training, it's better to avoid using ambiguous terms.

耐力运动、抗阻运动和冲刺运动是三种最常见的运动类型。耐力运动的特点是长时间低阻力的持续或间歇性的肌肉活动。例如，慢跑是持续的耐力运动，冬季两项是间歇性的耐力运动。抗阻运动是短时间大阻力的肌肉活动，举重是一种典型的抗阻运动。冲刺运动是短时间低阻力的最大肌肉活动，例如 50 m 的游泳竞赛。

根据运动过程中能量产生的主要方式，还可以将运动分为有氧运动和无氧运动。有氧运动时，机体主要是直接或间接地从需要氧气的代谢过程中获取能量；而无氧运动时，机体主要是从不需要氧气的代谢过程中获取能量。耐力运动是有氧运动，抗阻运动和冲刺运动通常是无氧运动。

任何类型的运动都在一定程度上同时依赖有氧代谢和无氧代谢过程的能量供应。但我们总是忽视"主要"这个词，导致人们认为运动可以是完全有氧的，或是完全无氧的。因此，当我们描述运动或训练时，最好避免使用模棱两可的术语。

7.2 Exercise Intensity
运动强度

Exercise intensity can be expressed by some quantitative indicators (Table 7.1). Heart rate is the easiest way to express exercise intensity. The percentage of maximum rate of oxygen uptake ($\dot{V}O_2max$) is a favorite measure of the relative intensity of exercise, particularly in endurance exercise. Sometimes, the percentage of maximum heart rate (HRmax=220–age) and the metabolic equivalent of task (MET) are also used to express the relative exercise intensity. The percentage of one-repetition maximum (1RM) is a favorite measure of resistance exercise. Rating of perceived exertion (RPE) is another useful measure of exercise intensity. It is a subjective rating scale used to assess the difficulty of exercise on a scale of 6 to 20.

运动强度可以用一些定量指标来表示（表7.1）。心率是表示运动强度的最简单的方式。最大摄氧量百分比（%V̇O₂max）是衡量运动相对强度的最常用的指标，尤其是在耐力运动中。此外，最大心率百分比（%HRmax，HRmax=220−年龄）和代谢当量（MET）也用来表示相对运动强度。最大肌力百分比（%1RM）适用于评价抗阻运动的强度。主观体力感觉（RPE）是另一种有用的运动强度测量方法，它是一种主观评定量表，用6~20的分值来评定运动的强度。

Table 7.1   The classification and evaluation of exercise intensity

Qualitative descriptor	%V̇O₂max	%HRmax	MET	%1RM	RPE
Light exercise	≤ 45	≤ 63	<3	<50	6–11
Moderate-intensity exercise	46–63	64–76	3–5.9	50–69	12–13
Hard, or vigorous exercise	64–90	77–95	6–8.7	70–84	14–17
Near-maximal to maximal exercise	≥ 91	≥ 96	≥ 8.8	≥ 85	18–20

In contrast to the quantitative description, there are also some qualitative descriptions, such as high, medium and low intensity. High-intensity exercise (HIE) can be defined as a maximal bout of exercise which lasts for less than one second (like a kick, jump, punch, or throw) or sustains 1–2 minutes. This includes events such as sprint track cycling, maximal running distances between 60–200 meters, 50–100 meters swimming, most field events in athletics, sprint ice-skating and so on. High-intensity intermittent exercise (HIIE) refers to the exercise that is characterized by fluctuations in exercise intensity over a given time. HIIE typically consists of repeated high-intensity activity (close to maximum or supra-maximum) interspersed with low to moderate intensity exercise, or in some cases completely inactive (rest). Soccer, basketball, rugby, tennis, boxing and hockey are HIIE.

相对于对运动强度的定量描述，也有一些定性描述，如高强度、中强度和低强度。高强度运动（HIE）可以定义为持续时间不超过1 s（如踢腿、跳跃、拳击或投掷）或1~2 min的最大肌肉活动。短跑、场地自行车、60~200 m的冲刺跑、50~100 m游泳、大多数田赛项目，以及短道滑冰等项目都属于高强度运动。高强度间歇性运动（HIIE）是指在一定时间内以运动强度波动为特征的最大肌肉活动。HIIE通常包括重复的高强度（接近最大或超最大）运动，中间穿插低到中强度的运动或在某些情况下完全不活动（休息）。足球、篮球、橄榄球、网球、拳击和曲棍球都属于是高强度间歇性运动。

7.3 Exercise Duration
运动持续时间

A movement that is performed only once is an acute exercise. A shorter period of exercise training is classified as short-term exercise. If the exercise is repeated regularly and lasts for more than three months, it is normally classified as long-term exercise.

Time is the only way to express the duration of each exercise. Sometimes we classify an exercise lasting up to one minute as short period, an exercise lasting more than ten minutes as prolonged period, and an exercise lasting between one and ten minutes as intermediate duration. But this is just a subjective classification. There is no uniform classification of exercise duration.

Endurance exercise can typically be defined as a prolonged steady-state exercise that lasts between four minutes and four hours. During endurance exercise, the exercise intensity is usually considered as steady state (constant intensity) in order to exercise at the highest power output for as long as possible. The most common modes of endurance exercise are cycling and running.

只进行一次的运动是单次运动，一般较短时间的运动被归类为短期运动，而三个月以上的规律运动才能被定义为长期运动。

时间是表示每次运动持续长度的唯一指标。有时，我们把持续 1 min 以内的运动定义为短时间运动，持续 1~10 min 的运动定义为中等时间的运动，持续 10 min 以上的运动定义为长时间运动。但这只是一种主观的分类方法，关于运动持续时间的分类还没有统一的标准。

耐力运动通常被定义为持续时间在 4 min~4 h 之间的长时间稳态运动。在耐力运动中，运动强度通常被认为是恒定的，以便以最高的输出功率进行尽可能长时间的运动。最常见的耐力运动方式是骑自行车和跑步。

7.4 Exercise Frequency
运动频率

If exercise is repeated regularly, the frequency is a parameter that affects the body's metabolic responses. There is no classification of exercise frequency. Athletes may train twice daily, while a person engaged in movement fitness may only train three times per week.

在有规律的重复运动中，运动频率也是影响机体代谢反应的一个重要的运动参数。运动频率没有分类，一个运动员可能每天训练两次，而一个进行运动健身的人可能每周训练三次。

Chapter 8 Energy for Exercise

第八章 运动中的能量来源

Chemical energy is a form of potential energy stored in the chemical bonds of biological molecules. Exergonic reaction (Energy–producing reaction) and endergonic reaction (energy–consuming reaction) are two chemical reactions in which energy exchange occurs in the body. Biomolecules are broken down into smaller molecules in the catabolism process, thereby providing raw materials for the synthesis of larger molecules, which are needed for body functions. Catabolism releases energy, part of which is used to synthesize ATP. In contrast to catabolism, cells need anabolism to grow, divide, replace worn-out molecules, and create an energy reservoir. Anabolism is an energy-consuming process (Figure 8.1).

化学能是储存在生物分子的化学键中的一种势能。释放能量的反应（产能反应）和吸收能量的反应（耗能反应）是发生在体内的两种能量交换的化学反应。生物分子在分解代谢过程中被分解成较小的分子，从而产生合成大分子的原料，这些大分子是机体发挥功能所需要的。分解代谢同时还释放能量，其中一部分用于再合成三磷酸腺苷（ATP）。与分解代谢相反，细胞需要合成代谢来满足生长、分裂过程中损耗分子的更替需要，并创建能量储存库。合成代谢是一个能量消耗的过程（图8.1）。

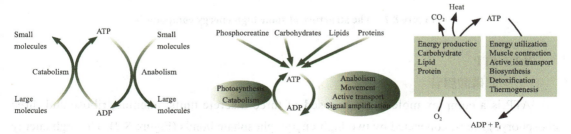

Figure 8.1 ATP -ADP Cycle

8.1 High-energy Phosphate Compounds
高能磷酸化合物

High–energy phosphate compounds (Compounds with high phosphoryl–transfer potential) are the first class of energy sources in exercise. They contain phosphoryl groups linked with high-energy phosphate bonds which release a large amount of free energy (>5 kcal/mol) during hydrolysis. The most common high-energy phosphate compounds are ATP, ADP and phosphocreatine (Figure 8.2).

高能磷酸化合物（高磷酸转移电位化合物）含有由高能磷酸键连接的磷酸基，是运动中的直接能量来源。在水解过程中，高能磷酸化合物可以释放大量的自由能（>5 kcal/mol）。最常见的高能磷酸盐化合物是三磷酸腺苷（ATP）、二磷酸腺苷（ADP）和磷酸肌酸（PCr）。（图 8.2）。

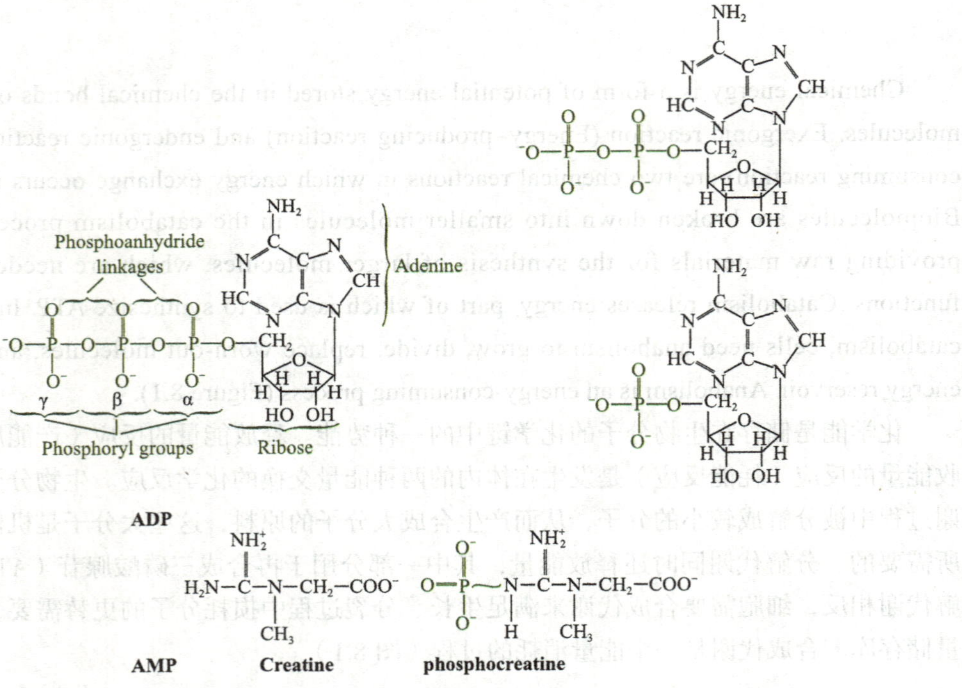

Figure 8.2   The structure of some high energy compounds

8.1.1 ATP
三磷酸腺苷

ATP is a complex molecule composed of three discrete units: adenine, ribose and three phosphoryl groups, connected by two high-energy phosphate bonds (Figure 8.2). The high energy content of ATP resides in the high-energy phosphate bonds, which hydrolyze one by one and release a large amount of free energy. The free energy released is transferred to the molecules that require energy to reach a higher level of activation. Therefore, ATP serves as an ideal energy-transfer agent.

ATP is a direct energy source for cells. In addition to ATP, the other ribonucleoside triphosphates (GTP, UTP, and CTP) are also direct energy sources. These energy sources represented by ATP are called energy currency.

ATP 是一种复杂的分子，由三个离散单元组成：腺嘌呤、核糖和由两个高能磷酸键连接的三个磷酸基（图 8.2）。ATP 所含高能量存在于高能磷酸键中，高能磷酸键一个接一个水解释放出大量的自由能，并直接转移到其他需要能量的分子中，使其达到更高的活化水平。因此，ATP 是理想的能量传递者。

ATP 是细胞的直接能量来源。除 ATP 外，其他的三磷酸核糖核酸，如三磷酸鸟苷（GTP）、三磷酸尿苷（UTP）、三磷酸胞苷（CTP）等，也是直接能源。这些直接能源，以 ATP 为代表，被称为能源货币。

8.1.2 ADP
二磷酸腺苷

ADP is the product of ATP hydrolysis, but it can be resynthesized into ATP again. The terminal phosphoryl group of one ADP is transferred to another ADP, converting the former to AMP and the latter to ATP, which is catalyzed by adenylate kinase (Figure 8.3). So energy is squeezed from ADP.

ADP 是 ATP 水解的产物，但它可以重新合成 ATP。在腺苷酸激酶的催化下，一个 ADP 的末端磷酸基转移到另一个 ADP，则前者转化为 AMP（腺苷–磷酸），后者转化为 ATP（图 8.3），这样能量就从 ADP 中释放出来了。

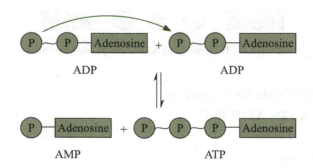

Figure 8.3　Squeezing energy out of ADP

8.1.3 Phosphocreatine
磷酸肌酸

Phosphocreatine (PCr) is the product of phosphorylation of creatine. A large amount of free energy is released when the bond between the creatine in phosphocreatine and phosphate molecules is broken. Phosphocreatine can efficiently be used to resynthesize ATP within 1–2 seconds of maximum muscle contraction. PCr can directly transfer high–energy phosphate group to ADP to synthesize ATP without oxygen (Figure 8.4). Thus, it is the fastest source for ATP resynthesis.

Since phosphocreatine has a greater free energy of hydrolysis than ATP, phosphorylation serves as a "reservoir" of high energy phosphate bonds. The hydrolysis of phosphorylation is catalyzed by the creatine kinase (4% to 6% on the outer mitochondrial membrane, 3% to 5% in the sarcomere, and 90% in the cytosol) to drive ADP phosphorylation to ATP. Cells store approximately four to six times more phosphocreatine than ATP. Phosphocreatine is a valuable source of energy during strenuous exercise.

磷酸肌酸（PCr）是肌酸磷酸化的产物。当磷酸肌酸的肌酸和磷酸盐分子之间的键断裂时，会释放大量的自由能。磷酸肌酸能在最大肌肉收缩的 1~2 s 有效地重新合成 ATP。PCr 可以在不需要氧气的情况下，将高能磷酸基团直接转移给 ADP 再合成 ATP（图 8.4），因此，PCr 是 ATP 重新合成最快的来源。

由于 PCr 比 ATP 具有更大的水解自由能，磷酸化就成为一个高能量磷酸键的"蓄水池"。磷酸水解由肌酸激酶催化（4%~6% 在线粒体膜外，3%~5% 在肌节，90% 在细胞质）驱动 ADP 磷酸化到 ATP。细胞储存的 PCr 为 ATP 的 4~6 倍。PCr 是极量运动中重要的能量来源。

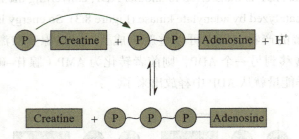

Figure 8.4　Replenishing ATP from phosphocreatine

8.2 ATP–ADP Cycle in Exercise
运动中的 ATP–ADP 循环

8.2.1 ATP–ADP Cycle
ATP–ADP 循环

In most cases, ATP is used as a direct energy source of anabolism, active transport, and signal amplification, but its storage capacity is limited (usually 20–30 mmol/kg dry muscle). In order to ensure that the body has continuous energy supplement, ATP and ADP participate in the ATP–ADP cycle. ATP, representative of energy currency, is broken down into ADP and Pi, providing energy for anabolism,, active transport, and signal amplification. ADP and Pi use the energy released by the catabolic processes to resynthesize ATP (Figure 8.1). The ATP–ADP cycle is the main route of energy exchange in biological systems.

In the cycle, ADP, phosphocreatine, carbohydrates, lipids, or proteins, are indirect energy sources (fuels) to supply (or replenish) for the energy of the cycle needed. ATP is both the energy donor and energy receiver. In general, the less ATP used, the less fuel is oxidized to generate ATP. Any increase in energy demand will immediately disrupt the balance between ATP, ADP and Pi. This imbalance condition will stimulate the breakdown of other stored energy-containing compounds to re-synthesize ATP.

ATP 是合成代谢、主动运输和信号放大等生物过程的直接能量来源，但其储量有限（通常为 20~30 mmol/kg 干肌）。为了保证机体有持续的能量补充，ATP 和 ADP 形成了 ATP-ADP 循环。ATP 是能量的直接来源，它被分解成 ADP 和 Pi（磷酸根离子），为合成代谢、主动运输和信号放大的过程提供能量。而 ADP 和 Pi 利用分解代谢过程释放的能量再合成 ATP（图 8.1）。ATP-ADP 循环是生物系统中能量交换的主要途径。

在 ATP-ADP 循环过程中，ADP、磷酸肌酸、糖类、脂类或蛋白质等都是再合成 ATP 的间接能量来源（燃料）。ATP 既是能量的供应者，也是能量的接受者。一般来说，使用的 ATP 越少，被氧化产生 ATP 的燃料就越少。任何能量需求的增加都会立即破坏 ATP、ADP 和 Pi 之间的平衡，这种不平衡刺激了其他储存能量的化合物的分解以再合成 ATP。

8.2.2 ATP-ADP Cycle in Exercise
运动中的 ATP-ADP 循环

Whether we are resting or exercising, the metabolic reactions that take place in the body are the same. The huge change that occurs when transitioning from one state to the other is the rate of reactions taking place: some reactions are accelerated, while others slow down, allowing the body to respond to the demands of each state. Exercise stimulates the processes of movement, active transport and signal amplification to accelerate the breakdown of ATP. For example, the energy output of active muscles exceeds their resting value by 120 times or more; during less intense but sustained marathon running, the whole-body energy requirement increases 20 to 30 times above resting levels.

Lower intensity exercise elicits a smaller decrease in ATP because of its lower energy demands. The decrease of ATP in long-duration exercise is smaller too, because the processes of regenerating ATP have more time to balance its breakdown. The ATP-ADP cycle creates a stable source of ATP to maintain and meet exercise needs. ATP storage will be completely depleted within a few seconds of maximum exercise. In fact, even during exhaustive exercise, muscle ATP storage will never be depleted by more than 20%–40%. It is reported that after 30 seconds of maximum cycling, phosphocreatine is reduced by 80%, as converted to creatine, and ATP is slightly reduced, with the increase of ADP and Pi (Figure 8.5).

无论我们是在休息还是在运动，体内发生的代谢反应都是一样的。从一种状态转换到另一种状态时，最引人注目的变化是化学反应速度的改变：一些反应加快，而另一些反应减慢，以确保机体能够对每种状态的需求做出反应。运动刺激了新陈代谢过程中需要消耗ATP的转运、主动运输和信号放大等过程，从而加速了ATP的消耗。例如，活动肌肉的能量消耗是静息时的120倍或更多；在强度较低但持续的马拉松跑步中，对全身能量的需求比休息时高出20~30倍。

ATP-ADP循环创造稳定的ATP来源以维持和满足运动的需要。低强度的运动会引起ATP的小幅度下降，因为它们对能量的需求更低；长时间运动中，ATP储量的下降幅度也较小，因为运动过程中有足够的时间再合成ATP来补充消耗的ATP；在高强度运动中，ATP储存会在几秒钟内完全耗尽，但事实上，即使在剧烈运动中，肌肉储存的ATP也不会消耗超过20%~40%。据报道，30 s最大速度自行车运动后，磷酸肌酸降低80%，肌酸含量增加，ATP略有下降，而ADP和Pi增加（图8.5）。

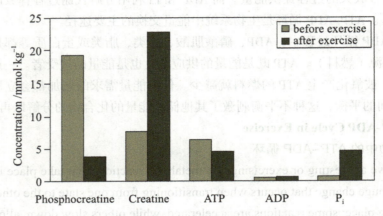

Figure 8.5　Changes in the concentrations of compounds related to
energy production during maximal exercise

8.3 Energy Supply System
能量供应系统

High-energy phosphates (ATP and phosphocreatine), carbohydrates, lipids and proteins serve as the sources of intramuscular energy in exercise. The catabolism of these substances for energy production is often referred to as energy metabolism. Limited ATP reserves provide a biologically effective mechanism to regulate energy metabolism.

运动中，高能磷酸化合物（ATP和PCr）、糖类、脂类和蛋白质是肌肉内的能量来源。这些物质分解产生能量的过程通常被称为能量代谢。有限的ATP储备提供了一种有效的能量代谢调节机制。

8.3.1 The Synthesize Types of ATP
ATP 的合成类型

ATP can be synthesized through two different chemical reaction processes: substrate-level phosphorylation and oxidative phosphorylation. Substrate-level phosphorylation is an anaerobic process in which ATP or another ribonucleoside triphosphate is synthesized using a high-energy phosphate compound as substrate. Oxidative phosphorylation is an aerobic metabolism process of macronutrients in mitochondria, which contributes energy to promote the resynthesis of ATP. About 40% of the potential energy in food nutrients is transferred to ATP, so most of the energy for phosphorylation derives from the oxidation of dietary carbohydrates, lipids, and proteins.

机体可以通过底物水平磷酸化和氧化磷酸化两种不同的化学反应过程来合成 ATP。底物水平磷酸化是一个厌氧过程，以一个高能量磷酸化合物为底物来合成 ATP 或另一个三磷酸核糖核苷；氧化磷酸化是大量营养物质在线粒体中通过有氧分解代谢释放能量以促进 ATP 重新合成的过程。食物营养素中大约 40% 的势能可以转化为 ATP，因此大部分用于磷酸化的能量来自膳食中的糖类、脂类和蛋白质的氧化。

8.3.2 The Energy Resynthesis Systems during Exercise
运动中的能量再合成系统

Cells contain a small quantity of ATP, so it must be continually re-synthesized to meet its average rate. There are three pathways to resynthesize ATP: ATP-phosphagen system, anaerobic glycolysis (lactate system) and aerobic system. Such pathways support our daily life. The energy provision for exercise is the smooth blending and overlapping of all three energy systems (Figure 8.6). Muscle cells have a highly coordinated and regulatory network in signal and feedback pathways which function to ensure the ATP demands and ATP synthesis.

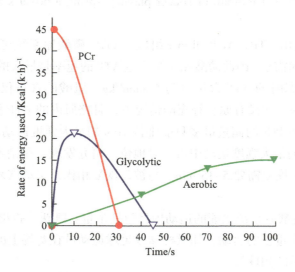

Figure 8.6 Energy continuum of exercise

细胞中仅含有少量的 ATP，因此必须按照消耗的速度不断地重新合成 ATP。ATP 的重新合成有三种途径：ATP–磷酸原系统、糖无氧酵解系统（乳酸系统）和有氧系统，以满足机体日常的能量需求。运动训练中的能量供应依赖三个能量系统的交互作用（图 8.6）。肌肉细胞具有高度协调的信号调节网络和反馈通路以确保 ATP 的需求与 ATP 的合成相匹配。

8.3.2.1 ATP–phosphagen System

ATP–磷酸原系统

ATP–phosphagen system is composed of ATP, ADP, and phosphocreatine. The ATP–phosphagen system shows an almost instantaneous capacity to match ATP demand in a swift supply, thus the phosphagen system has the maximal rate of ATP production, which is twice as fast as that of glycolysis.

Skeletal muscle at rest state contains only about 6 mmol/kg ATP, 12 mmol/kg creatine and 20 mmol/kg phosphocreatine. It is estimated that, in the absence of sources, ATP will deplete in about 3 seconds of maximum exercise and the dominance of phosphocreatine does not exceed 10 seconds of maximum exercise. Therefore, the ATP-phosphagen system can predominate about 10 seconds of maximum exercise. After exercise, it may take 5–15 minutes for the PCr to fully recover. Compared with passive recovery, active recovery appears to promote much faster in PCr regeneration.

Activities that heavily rely on the phosphagen system to provide ATP include weightlifting, jumping, throwing, 60-meter sprint, and any other high–intensity exercise repeated multiple bouts in a short duration, such as a football or soccer player's sprint, a boxer's attack, and a spike in volleyball.

ATP–磷酸原系统由 ATP、ADP 和 PCr 组成。ATP–磷酸原系统可在瞬间提供 ATP 来满足机体对 ATP 的快速需求，因此磷酸原系统产生 ATP 的速率是最大的，是糖酵解的两倍。

骨骼肌在静息状态时的 ATP 含量仅为 6 mmol/kg，肌酸的含量仅为 12 mmol/kg，PCr 的含量仅为 20 mmol/kg。在没有原料补充的情况下，骨骼肌内的 ATP 储量仅能维持 3 s 左右的最大强度运动，而 PCr 的储量最多只能维持 10 s 的最大强度运动。因此，ATP–磷酸原系统在持续约 10 s 的最大强度运动中占主导地位。研究发现，在剧烈、高强度运动后，被消耗的磷酸肌酸完全恢复需要 5~15 min。与被动恢复相比，主动恢复更有利于磷酸肌酸的快速再生。

主要依靠 ATP–磷酸原系统供能的运动项目包括举重、跳跃、投掷、60 m 短跑和任何其他短时间高强度动作重复的运动，如橄榄球或足球运动员在赛场上的冲刺跑、拳击运动员的攻击和排球运动员的扣球等。

8.3.2.2 Anaerobic Glycolysis (Lactate System)

糖无氧酵解系统（乳酸系统）

Anaerobic glycolysis (Lactate system) occurs in the aqueous medium of cells outside the mitochondrion and results in lactate formation (Glycogen → Glucose-1-P → Lactic acid + ATP).

Anaerobic glycolysis is an alternative pathway that can regenerate ATP in a rapid rate during the high-intensity exercise. Glycolysis of one molecule of glucose generates a net of 2 ATP molecules by substrate–level phosphorylation. However, the degradation of glycogen to produce one glucose molecule for glycolysis, it produces a net of 3 ATP.

Once the muscle starts to contract, the process of anaerobic glycolysis begins. Anaerobic glycolysis does not contribute energy to as much as to PCr in the short term, but its contribution is likely to predominate within 10–60 seconds. The major substrate of anaerobic glycolysis is glycogen. Therefore, in the absence of adequate glycogen supplementation, early vigorous exercise will limit the subsequent high-intensity short term exercise.

Activities that heavily rely on ATP generated by anaerobic glycolysis include 100, 200, and 400 meter runs, the 50 and 100 meter swimming, and the 200, 500, and 1,000 meter cycling races.

糖无氧酵解系统的代谢过程（糖原→1- 磷酸 – 葡萄糖→乳酸 +ATP）发生在线粒体外的细胞质中，生成乳酸。在高强度运动中，糖无氧酵解是一种快速再合成 ATP 的替代途径。一个葡萄糖分子的酵解过程通过底物水平磷酸化可以净生成 2 个 ATP 分子，而糖原降解生成一个葡萄糖分子可净生成 3 个 ATP。

一旦肌肉开始收缩，糖无氧酵解的过程就开始了。糖无氧酵解在短期内的能量贡献不如 PCr 大，但其作用可能在 10~60 s 内占主导地位。糖无氧酵解的主要底物是糖原，因此，在没有充分糖原补充的情况下，前期的剧烈运动将限制后续的短时间高强度运动。

主要依靠糖无氧酵解系统获得 ATP 的运动项目包括：100 m、200 m 和 400 m 的跑步，50 m、100 m 游泳，还有 200 m、500 m 和 1000 m 自行车赛。

8.3.2.3 Aerobic system (Oxygen System)

有氧系统

The energy sources of aerobic system include carbohydrates, lipids, and proteins. Energy released by the aerobic catabolism of macronutrients is divided into three stages: ① broken down into their monomers; ② converted into acetyl-CoA and produced a small amount of ATP; ③ oxidized to carbon dioxide (CO_2) and H_2O in the citric acid cycle, and produced much more ATP (Figure 8.7).

有氧系统的供能物质包括糖类、脂类和蛋白质。这些宏量营养素通过有氧分解代谢释放能量的过程可以分为三个阶段：①分解为基本结构单位；②转化为乙酰辅酶 A，并产生少量的 ATP；③在柠檬酸循环中氧化成二氧化碳和水，产生大量的 ATP（图 8.7）。

The aerobic system produces the largest amount of ATP molecules. For example, the complete decomposition of a glucose molecule into carbon dioxide and water will produce a net gain of 32 ATP; a triacylglycerol molecule composed of three18-carbon fatty acid molecules is able to net generate 460 ATP. But the rate of ATP production is considerably slower than the ATP-phosphagen system or glycolysis.

During the exercise lasting more than 60 minutes, such as long-distance run, marathons, ultra long-distance run, the ATP provided by the aerobic system have gradually become the main energy source. The recovery period of all exercises mainly relies on ATP generated by aerobic system.

在有氧系统中 ATP 的生成量是最大的，例如，一个葡萄糖分子完全分解为二氧化碳和水可以净生成 32 个 ATP；一个由 3 个 18- 碳脂肪酸分子组成的三酰甘油，可以净生成 460 个 ATP。但是有氧系统产生 ATP 的速度比 ATP- 磷酸系统或糖无氧酵解系统要慢很多。

持续时间在 60 min 以上的运动，如长跑、马拉松、超级长跑等，有氧系统提供的 ATP 逐渐成为主要的能量来源。所有运动的恢复期都主要依靠于有氧系统产生的 ATP。

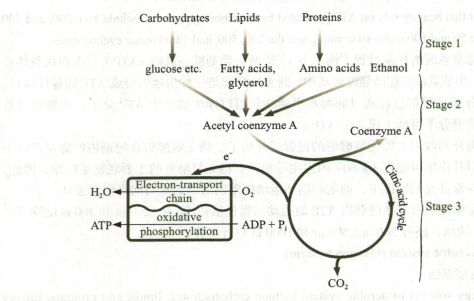

Figure 8.7   Stages of aerobic catabolism

All exercise is fueled by multiple sources of energy (rather than a single source), especially carbohydrates and fats. Fat contributes a greater percentage of energy in lower-intensity exercise and recovery. Carbohydrate contributes a greater percentage of energy in higher-intensity exercise (Figure 8.8).

所有的运动都是由多个供能物质（而不是单一的来源）提供能量的，其中糖类和脂肪的供能作用更突出。在较低强度的运动和恢复中，脂肪的供能比例较高，高强度、长时间的运动则糖类供能比例较高（图 8.8）。

8.3.3 The Synergy of Energy Resynthesis Systems
供能系统的协同作用

In contrast to aerobic pathway, the ATP-phosphagen system and anaerobic glycolysis are called the anaerobic pathway, and they are independent of oxygen. There are fundamental

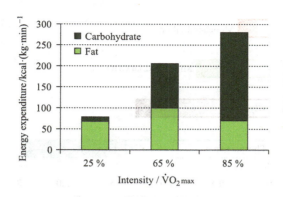

Figure 8.8 Carbohydrate and fat use at three exercise intensities

differences among the three energy systems. The aerobic pathway can produce a large amount of ATP, but the production speed is slow, so it is also called the long-term energy system; while the anaerobic pathway produces a limited amount of ATP, but the production speed is very fast, so it is also called the immediate and short-term energy system (Figure 8.9). The contribution percentage of the energy systems to the total energy supply in muscle depends on the duration and intensity of maximum exercise (Figure 8.10, Figure 8.11, Table 8.1). Typically, as exercise intensity proceeds from moderate (65% $\dot{V}O_2$max) to high-intensity (85% $\dot{V}O_2$max), muscle glycogenolysis increases and glucose uptake rises, so that carbohydrate (CHO) metabolism predominates. In contrast, systemic lipid oxidation seems to be reduced due to reduced free fat acid (FFA) in plasma and intramuscular triglyceride oxidation. The maximum rate of lipid oxidation is considered to be occurred around 65% $\dot{V}O_2$max, depending on many other factors such as training status, gender and diet.

一般情况下，相对于有氧系统，代谢过程不依赖氧气的 ATP–磷酸原系统和糖无氧酵解系统称为无氧系统。这三个能量供应系统之间有着本质的区别：有氧供能系统可产生大量的 ATP，但生成速度缓慢，所以又称为长期供能系统；而无氧系统产生的 ATP 数量虽然有限，但生成速度快，因此也称为直接和短期供能系统（图8.9）。各供能系统对肌肉总能量供应的贡献率取决于最大运动的持续时间和强度（图8.10、图8.11、表8.1）。通常，当运动强度从中等强度（65% $\dot{V}O_2$max）增加到高强度（85% $\dot{V}O_2$max）时，肌肉糖原分解和葡萄糖摄取增加，糖类作为主要的供能物质；相反，由于血浆游离脂肪酸（FFA）和肌内甘油三酯氧化率降低，全身脂肪氧化减少。脂肪氧化的最大速率被认为在 65% $\dot{V}O_2$max 左右，但取决于许多其他因素，如训练状态、性别和饮食等。

It is hard to say any kind of exercise that can obtain energy from only one energy supply system. The energy provision for exercise is a smooth blend and overlap of all three energy systems (Figure 8.12). Two or more synthesis pathways contribute to energy resynthesis,

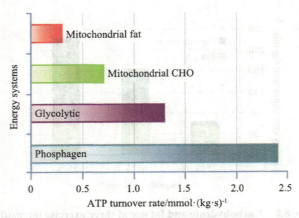

Figure 8.9　Maximum rate of ATP regeneration

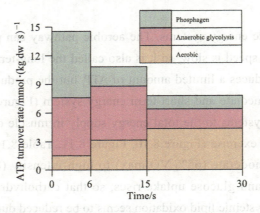

Figure 8.10　Effect of duration of maximal exercise on substrate use and rate of ATP turnover

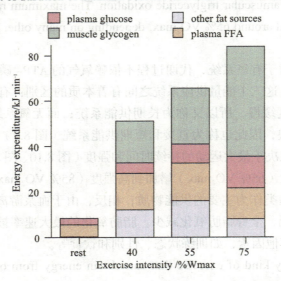

Figure 8.11　Effects of exercise intensity on substrate utilization during exercise

Table 8.1 Contributions of various energy resynthesis systems during different durations and intensities

Duration	Intensity	Primary Energy System
0–5 seconds	Maximal effort	Phosphagen system（predominantly）
6–30 seconds	Very intense	Phosphagen system（becoming depleted around 10 sec） Glycolysis（assuming primary role）
30–120 seconds	Intense	Glycolysis（predominantly）
2–3 minutes	Moderate	Glycolysis（becoming depleted） Aerobic system（assuming primary role）
>3 minutes	Lower	Oxidative（almost exclusively）

depending on the exercise parameters, characteristics of the exerciser, and environmental factors. During low-intensity exercise (20%–60% $\dot{V}O_2max$), ATP resynthesis primarily comes from aerobic metabolism in the mitochondria. In particular, lipid catabolism makes a substantial contribution to ATP resynthesis at this intensity. However, when exercise intensity approaches approximately 60% $\dot{V}O_2max$, lipid catabolism decreases significantly. Gradually, the body begins to favor the oxidation of carbohydrates in the mitochondria. Carbohydrates are a more efficient fuel. Consuming one muscle oxygen, carbohydrates can produce much more ATP quickly. As the intensity continues to increase, the contribution of glycolysis steadily increases. When approaching maximum exercise, the phosphagen system is involved in energy supply to produce the most ATP at a fast rate. Although glycolysis and the phosphagen system are activated during higher intensity exercise, mitochondrial aerobic metabolism are continuously activated, and make a significant contribution to overall ATP production.

　　没有任何一种运动能够只从一种供能系统获得能量，运动中的能量供应是三个供能系统的协同作用（图 8.12）。根据运动参数、运动者的特征和环境因素，有两种或两种以上的合成途径参与能量的再合成。在整个低强度运动范围内（20%~60% $\dot{V}O_2max$），ATP 的供应主要来自线粒体内的有氧代谢，特别是脂肪分解代谢产生的 ATP 在这个运动强度范围有实质性的贡献。然而，随着运动强度增大并接近 60% $\dot{V}O_2max$，脂肪分解供能比例明显降低，渐渐地身体开始倾向于使用糖的氧化供能。糖类是一种效率更高的燃料，消耗一分子氧气可以更快、更多地生成 ATP。随着运动强度的继续增加，糖无氧酵解的供能比例持续增加，在接近最大强度时，磷酸原系统也参与供能，以最大限度地产生 ATP。尽管在较高强度的运动中，糖无氧酵解系统和磷酸原系统的活性提高了，但线粒体的有氧代谢仍持续升高，并对 ATP 的总体生成做出了显著贡献。

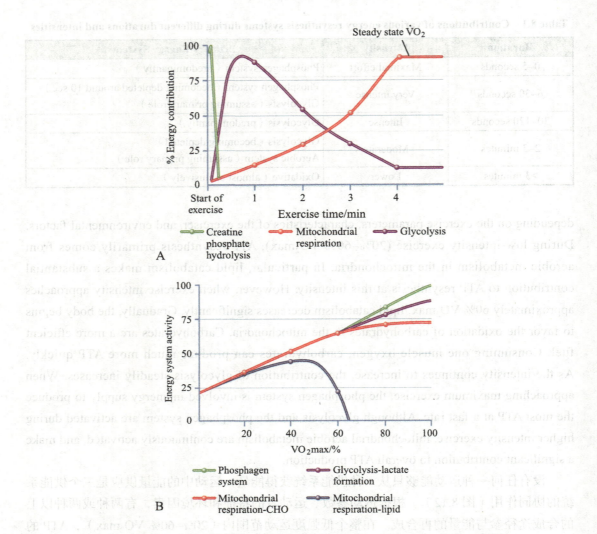

**Figure 8.12   The contributions of energy systems during different durations (A)
and the sequential overlapping of energy systems for high–intensity exercise (B)**

8.3.4 The Storage of Energy Sources
供能物质的储备

In the body, the liver provides a rich source of amino acids and glucose, while adipocytes generate a large number of energy-rich fatty acid molecules. After their release, the blood stream delivers these compounds to the muscle cells (Figure 8.13).

在人体内，肝脏可以提供丰富的氨基酸和葡萄糖，而脂肪细胞产生大量的能量丰富的脂肪酸分子。供能物质释放入血后，血液将这些化合物输送到肌细胞（图 8.13）。

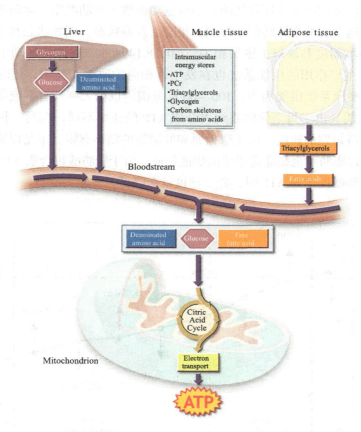

Figure 8.13   Pathway of ATP resynthesis in human body

8.4 Energy Supply Systems and Exercise
能量供应系统与运动

The contribution of each available energy source for the demands of exercise depends on exercise parameters (including exercise type, intensity, duration and frequency), the characteristics of the exerciser (including gender, age, nutritional status, training status and genome), and environmental factors (including ambient temperature and hypoxia). For example, the major energy source for running events at different distances is changed (Figure 8.14). Short-distance, high−intensity sprinting uses PCr predominantly, while the 100 m to 400 m events mainly use anaerobic glycolysis, and then aerobic metabolism predominates. Because each energy source re-synthesizes ATP at a different rate, it is impossible for athletes to maintain a sprint speed in a marathon. Because the storage of muscle and liver glycogen is limited to meet the energy needs of a full marathon, fatty acid is very important in energy production. The ATP resynthesis rate of fatty acids is slowest, thus the running speed will decrease.

运动中每种供能物质所发挥作用的大小与运动参数（运动类型、运动强度、持续时间和运动频率）、运动者的个体特征（性别、年龄、营养状态、训练状态和遗传特性）和环境因素（包括环境温度和缺氧）密切相关。如图 8.14 所示，在跑步运动中，随着跑动距离的变化，发挥主要作用的供能系统也在发生着相应的改变。其中，短时间、高强度的短跑以 ATP– 磷酸原系统供能为主，100~400 m 范围内以糖无氧酵解系统供能为主，随后采用有氧系统供能。由于每个供能系统再合成 ATP 的速率不同，在马拉松比赛中，运动员不可能始终保持短跑的速度。由于肌糖原和肝糖原的储存有限，不足以满足马拉松全程的能量需要，所以脂肪酸也是非常重要的供能物质。由于脂肪酸再合成 ATP 的速度最慢，因此，当利用脂肪酸提供的 ATP 时，跑步速度就会降低。

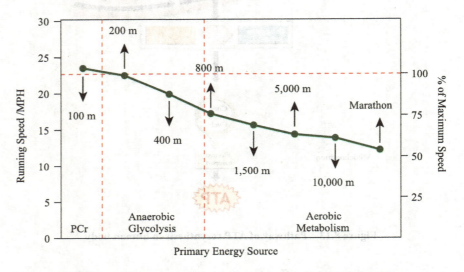

Figure 8.14　Primary energy sources for different running distances

Many types of sports (such as ball games) are characterized by high-intensity activity, which are intermittent with rest, light exercise, or moderate-intensity exercise. Under this circumstance, the proportion of energy sources exhibits great fluctuatios in a short period of time. The shorter the interval, the more prominent these changes.

There are gender differences in energy consumption during exercise. Compared with men, women's $\dot{V}O_2$max is lower because of the smaller heart volume, lower blood hemoglobin concentration, and lower percentage of muscle mass. Therefore, women oxidize more lipids and less carbohydrates and proteins when exercising at the same relative exercise intensity (Figure 8.15).

许多运动项目（如球类运动）的特点是高强度间歇性运动，运动间歇穿插着休息、轻度运动或中等强度的运动。在这种情况下，供能物质的供能比例在很短的时间内会表现出很大的波动，间隔越短，这些变化就越明显。

运动中供能物质的消耗存在性别差异。与男性相比，女性的最大摄氧量较低，这是因为她们心脏较小，血红蛋白浓度较低，肌肉质量百分比也较低。因此，以相同的相对强度运动时，女性消耗的脂肪更多，而消耗的糖类和蛋白质相对较少（图 8.15）。

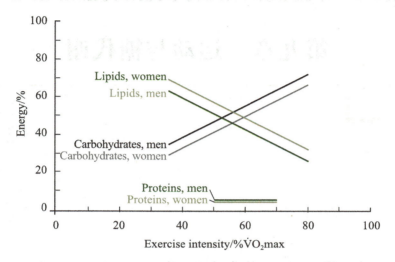

Figure 8.15   Sexes difference in the choice of energy sources during exercise

Based on limited research on the influence of ambient temperature, we cannot draw a definite conclusion on whether or how ambient temperature affects the proportion of energy sources during exercise. Some studies reported that doing exercise in the heat (about 40°C) will increases the proportion of carbohydrate to lipid oxidation compared to exercise at a neutral temperature (about 20°C). Other studies reported that doing exercise in the heat or in cold condition does not affect the choice of energy sources.

基于对环境温度影响的研究有限，我们无法得出一个确切的结论，即环境温度是否影响或如何影响运动期间的供能物质的供能比例。一些研究报告称，与在一般温度（约 20℃）下运动相比，在高温（约 40℃）下运动会增加糖类和脂类氧化的比例；另一些研究则报告称，在高温或低温下运动不会影响机体对供能物质的选择。

Chapter 9　Carbohydrate Metabolism in Exercise

第九章　运动与糖代谢

As mentioned in Chapter 1, carbohydrates, the energy source and primary metabolic substance, are closely related to the body's energy metabolism and exercise performance.

如第一章所述，糖类作为能量来源和代谢引物，其与机体的能量代谢和运动表现密切相关。

9.1 Carbohydrate Metabolism
糖代谢

From the schematic of energy production from carbohydrate in a muscle cell (Figure 9.1), we can see that glucose from glycogen and blood can be used to provide energy in the form of ATP at the muscle's cross bridge through anaerobic or aerobic processes.

从肌细胞糖类产生能量的示意图（图 9.1）中，我们可以看到糖原分解的葡萄糖和血液中的葡萄糖经由无氧或有氧代谢过程在肌肉横桥产生 ATP。

9.1.1 Glycogenesis and Glycogenolysis
糖原合成与分解

Glycogenesis is the formation of glycogen from glucose, which is regulated by glycogen synthase. Glycogen synthesis depends on the body's need for glucose and ATP (energy). If glucose level is high and the energy supply is adequate, insulin will promote the conversion of glucose into glycogen for storage in the liver and muscle cells (Figure 9.2).

糖原合成是由糖原合成酶调节的葡萄糖合成糖原的过程。糖原的合成取决于机体对葡萄糖和能量供应的需求。如果葡萄糖含量较高且机体能量供应充足，那么胰岛素就会促进葡萄糖合成糖原并储存在肝脏和肌肉中（图 9.2）。

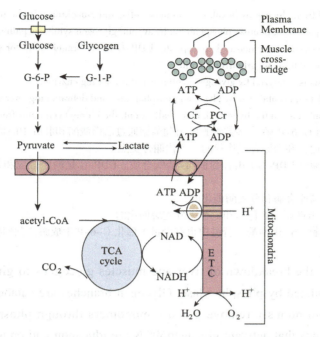

Figure 9.1 Schematic of energy production from carbohydrate in a muscle cell

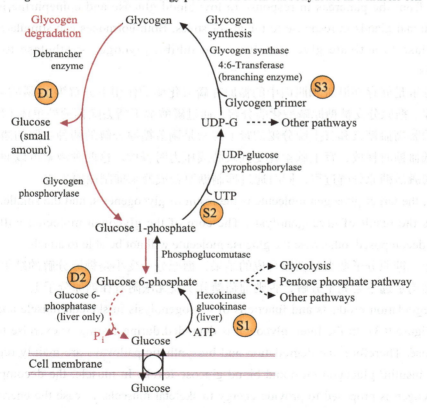

Figure 9.2 Glycogenesis and Glycogenolysis

S1: G–6–P is formed from glucose by hexokinase in most cells, and glucokinase in the liver. It is the metabolic branch point of glycolysis pathways, pentose phosphate pathway, and glycogen synthesis pathway.

S2: UDP–G is synthesized from glucose–1–phosphate. UDP–G is the branch point for glycogen synthesis and other pathways that require additional carbohydrate units.

S3: Glycogen synthesis is catalyzed by glycogen synthase and branching enzyme.

D1: Glycogen degradation is catalyzed by glycogen phosphorylase and debranching enzyme.

D2: Glucose–6–phosphatase in the liver (and, to a small extent, the kidney) generates free glucose from G–6–P.

S1: 葡萄糖–6–磷酸(G–6–P)在大多数细胞中由葡萄糖通过己糖激酶和肝脏中的葡萄糖激酶催化合成。它是糖酵解、磷酸戊糖途径和糖原合成途径的一个代谢分支点。

S2: 尿苷二磷酸葡糖（UDP–G）由葡萄糖–1–磷酸合成。UDP–G 是糖原合成和其他需要增加糖单位的代谢途径的分支点。

S3: 糖原合成是由糖原合酶和分支酶催化的。

D1: 糖原的降解是由糖原磷酸化酶和一种去分支酶催化的。

D2: 肝脏中的葡萄糖 –6– 磷酸酶（肾脏中也有少量）催化 G–6–P 生成游离葡萄糖。

Glycogenolysis, the breakdown of liver and muscles glycogens to glucose-1-phosphate and glycogen, is regulated by phosphorylase. Glycogen branches are catabolized by glycogen phosphorylase to continuously remove glucose monomers through phosphorolysis (Figure 9.2). The two hormones that activate glycogenolysis are glucagon and epinephrine. Glucagon is released from the pancreas in response to low blood glucose and epinephrine is released from the adrenal glands in response to threats or stress. Both hormones can stimulate glycogen phosphorylase to activate glycogenolysis and inhibit glycogen synthetase to suppress glycogenesis.

糖原分解是储存在肝脏和肌肉中的糖原在磷酸化酶的作用下分解为 1–磷酸–葡萄糖和糖原的过程。糖原分支被糖原磷酸化酶分解，通过磷酸解不断去除葡萄糖单体（图 9.2 ）。胰腺分泌的胰高血糖素和肾上腺分泌的肾上腺素是调节糖原分解的两种主要的激素。胰高血糖素在低血糖时释放，肾上腺素在受到威胁或压力时释放。这两种激素可以通过刺激糖原磷酸化酶激活糖原分解过程，同时通过抑制糖原合成酶来抑制糖原生成。

In fact, the larger glycogen molecule is the result of glycogenesis, and the smaller glycogen molecule is the result of glycogenolysis. The core of the glycogen molecule will never be completely decomposed, otherwise the glucose molecule will not be able to attach.

实际上，糖原分子变大是糖原合成的结果，糖原分子变小是糖原分解的结果。糖原分子的核心结构永远不会完全分解，否则葡萄糖分子就无法附着在糖原分子上。

The degradation products and functions of glycogenolysis in skeletal muscle and liver are different (Figure 9.3). In the liver, glycogen is degraded during fasting or exercise to stabilize blood glucose. Therefore, the degradation and biosynthetic pathways are mainly regulated by changes of insulin/ glucagon ratio and blood glucose levels. In muscle, the decomposition of hepatic glycogen is proposed to provide energy to skeletal muscels. In case the energy demand cannot be fulfilled by the hepatic glycogen, skeletal muscels are able to take in glucose in the blood generated hepatic glycogen.

　　糖原分解在骨骼肌和肝脏中的降解产物和功能是不同的（图9.3）。在肝脏中，糖原在空腹或运动期间为稳定血糖而降解。因此，肝糖原的降解和生物合成途径主要受胰岛素/胰高血糖素比值的变化和血糖水平的调节。而在肌肉中，糖原降解是为了给骨骼肌提供能量。当肌糖原不能满足能量需求时，骨骼肌会摄取肝糖原分解入血的葡萄糖（血糖）。

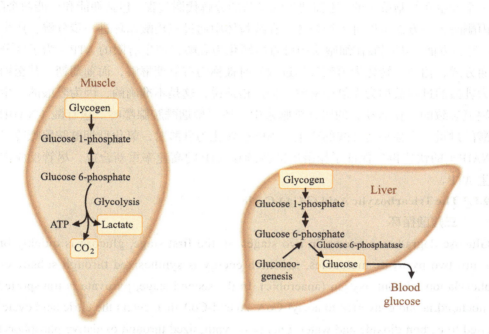

Figure 9.3　Glycogenolysis in skeletal muscle and liver

9.1.2 Glycolysis

　　糖酵解

Glycolysis is a series of ten reactions that extract energy from glucose by splitting it into two three-carbon molecules called pyruvate (Figure 9.4). Glycolysis is an anaerobic catabolic process that doesn't require oxygen and takes place in the cytosol of a cell. Glycolysis can be broken down into two main phases: the energy-requiring phase and the energy-releasing phase. On one hand, the glycolytic product, pyruvate, can enter the mitochondria, and further break down through the tricarboxylic acid cycle to produce a large amount of ATP; on the other hand, pyruvate can be directly converted into lactate in the cytoplasm and produce a small amount of ATP. In order to distinguish these two ways of metabolism, the conversion of glucose to pyruvates is sometimes called aerobic glycolysis, and the conversion of glucose (or even glycogen) into lactate is sometimes termed anaerobic glycolysis. But strictly speaking, this is not so accurate, because the production of lactate is not due to a lack of oxygen. In the cytosol of active muscle fibers, the overproduction of reduced nicotinamide adenine dinucleotide(NADH) and pyruvate accelerates the production of lactate. Due to the conversion of pyruvate to lactic acid, the fast regeneration of nicotinamide adenine dinucleotide (NAD^+) ensures the continued high speed of glycolysis and ATP resynthesis, even though the reaction itself does not produce ATP.

糖酵解是将1分子葡萄糖分解为2分子的丙酮酸并释放能量的10步系列反应（图9.4）。这是一个发生在细胞质中的，不需要氧气参与的分解代谢过程，包括耗能和产能两个阶段。产物丙酮酸，一方面可以进入线粒体，在线粒体中通过三羧酸循环进一步分解，产生大量ATP；另一方面，丙酮酸在细胞质中可直接转化为乳酸，产生有限的ATP。为了区分这两种代谢方式，葡萄糖转化为丙酮酸的过程有时被称为有氧糖酵解，而葡萄糖（甚至糖原）转化为乳酸的过程被称为无氧糖酵解。但严格地说，这是不准确的，因为乳酸的产生不是由于缺氧导致的。在运动肌的肌纤维胞浆中，还原型烟酰胺腺嘌呤二核苷酸（NADH）和丙酮酸的过量产生会加速乳酸的产生。丙酮酸转化为乳酸时，氧化型烟酰胺腺嘌呤二核苷酸（NAD^+）的快速再生保证了糖酵解的持续和ATP的高速率重新合成，尽管反应本身并不产生ATP。

9.1.3 The Tricarboxylic Acid (TCA) Cycle

三羧酸循环

Glucose degradation occurs in two stages. In the first stage, glucose is quickly broken down into two pyruvate molecules, in which energy is synthesized through substrate-level phosphorylation without oxygen (anaerobic). In the second stage, pyruvate is transported into the mitochondria and converted to acetyl-CoA, Acetyl-CoA then enters the citric acid cycle to be converted to carbon dioxide and water. Energy is synthesized through oxidative phosphorylation accompanied by electron transfer (Figure 9.4).

The citric acid cycle, also known as the tricarboxylic acid (TCA) cycle or Krebs cycle, is a series of enzymatic reactions that take place in the mitochondria (Figure 9.5). Sir Krebs outlined the 9 steps of the cycle in 1937. Although the TCA cycle does not directly use oxygen, it only works in the presence of oxygen. The TCA cycle is an open system that provides intermediates for many important anabolic reactions. The TCA cycle is the final pathway to release usable energy from the carbohydrates, proteins, and fats that we eat.

葡萄糖的降解分为两个阶段：第一阶段，葡萄糖迅速分解成两个丙酮酸分子，能量以不需要氧气参与的底物水平磷酸化的方式生成。第二阶段，丙酮酸进入线粒体，并转化为乙酰辅酶A，然后进入柠檬酸循环进一步氧化分解为二氧化碳和水，能量以伴随电子传递的氧化磷酸化方式生成（图9.4）。

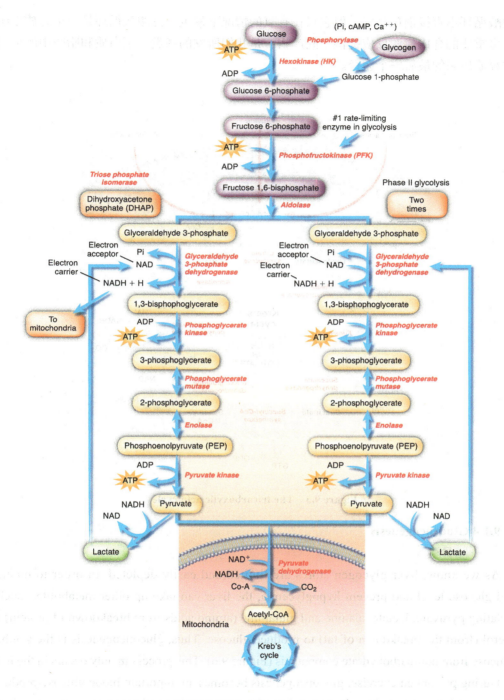

Figure 9.4　The glycolysis

柠檬酸循环又称三羧酸循环（TCA）或克雷布斯循环（克氏循环），是发生在线粒体内的系列酶促反应（图9.5）。克雷布斯爵士在1937年概述了这个循环的9个步骤。虽然三羧酸循环不直接消耗氧气，但它只在有氧的情况下发生。三羧酸循环是一个开放系统，为许多重要的合成代谢反应提供中间产物，是我们所吃的糖类、蛋白质和脂肪中的可用能量被释放出来的最后一个途径。

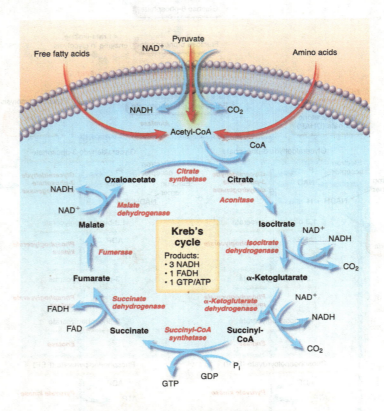

Figure 9.5　The tricarboxylic acid cycle

9.1.4 Gluconeogenesis
糖异生

As we know, liver glycogen stores are limited and easily depleted. In order to maintain blood glucose level and prevent hypoglycemia, the liver can take up other metabolites, such as circulating pyruvate, lactate, alanine and glutamine (amino acids from breakdown of protein) and glycerol (from the breakdown of fat) to produce glucose. Thus, gluconeogenesis is the synthesis of glucose from non-carbohydrate compounds (Figure 9.6). This process mainly occurs in the liver.

During prolonged exercise, gluconeogenesis becomes an important blood glucose-producing process, and it is promoted by decrease of insulin concentration and increase of glucagon levels. During endurance exercise, gluconeogenesis occurs if there is no intake of carbohydrate for 30–45 minutes.

正如我们所知，肝糖原储存有限，很容易耗尽。为了维持血糖水平，防止低血糖，肝脏可以利用其他物质，如循环中的丙酮酸、乳酸、丙氨酸、谷氨酰胺（蛋白质分解产生的氨基酸）和甘油（脂肪分解产生的）来产生葡萄糖。因此，葡萄糖异生是指从非糖类化合物中合成葡萄糖的过程（图9.6），这个过程主要发生在肝脏中。

在长时间的运动中，糖异生成为一个重要的血糖生成过程，胰岛素浓度降低和胰高血糖素水平升高会促进糖异生。在持续运动30~45 min后，只要不摄入含糖食物或饮料，糖异生过程就会发生。

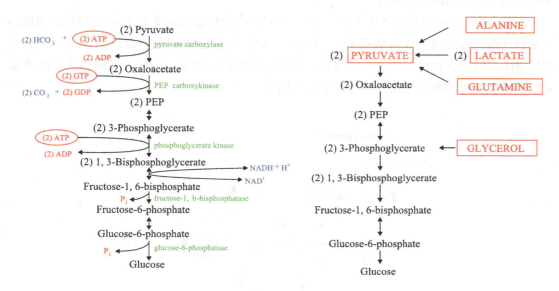

Figure 9.6 Gluconeogenesis

9.2 Exercise and Carbohydrate Metabolism in Muscle
运动与骨骼肌的糖代谢

9.2.1 Exercise and the Glycogenolysis in Muscle
运动与骨骼肌糖原分解

In muscle, glycogen is degraded to produce ATP. Thus, muscle glycogenolysis is mainly regulated by adenosine monophosphate (AMP), which signals a lack of ATP, and by Ca^{2+} released during contraction. The epinephrine, which is released in response to exercise and other stress situations, also activates skeletal muscle glycogenolysis. Thus, the rate of glycogenolysis in resting muscles is lower, but will be speeded up by exercise (Figure 9.7).

The degree of muscle glycogen depletion primarily depends on the initial glycogen content, exercise intensity, and exercise duration. For example, after one hour of vigorous exercise, the average reduction of muscle glycogen ranges from 40% (with high glycogen content) to 50% (with normal glycogen content). The rate of glycogen utilization is substantially higher during a 5,000 meter run rather than a marathon, but the glycogen depletion during a 5,000 meter race is not a concern because of the shorter duration.

When catabolized anaerobically, glycogen is the fastest source of ATP resynthesis ranked next to phosphocreatine, but it can regenerate much more ATP than phosphocreatine. In order to improve the energy efficiency of muscle glycogen, athletes must train themselves to avoid any purposeless breakdown of glycogen, and on the other hand, they must ensure rapid and massive mobilization at the time of need.

在肌肉中，糖原降解以产生 ATP，因此，骨骼肌中的糖原分解主要由腺苷 – 磷酸（AMP）含量和骨骼肌收缩过程中释放的 Ca^{2+} 的调节。AMP 含量增加是 ATP 缺乏的信号。在运动和其他压力情况下释放的肾上腺素也可以激活骨骼肌糖原分解，因此，与静息肌肉的糖原分解率相比，运动肌中的糖原分解率增加（图 9.7）。

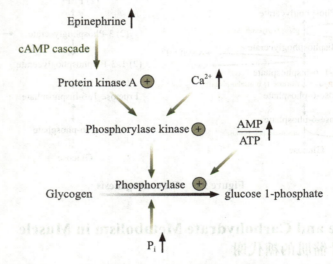

Figure 9.7   Control of glycogenolysis in muscle during exercise

骨骼肌糖原的消耗程度主要取决于初始糖原含量、运动强度和运动持续时间。例如，经过 1 h 的剧烈运动，肌肉中糖原含量平均减少 40%（高糖原储量）到 50%（正常糖原储量）。在 5000 m 的跑步中，糖原的利用率比马拉松要高得多，由于比赛时间较短，在 5000 m 的比赛中，糖原的消耗并不令人担心。

在无氧分解代谢过程中，糖原是仅次于磷酸肌酸的 ATP 重新合成的原料，而且糖原比磷酸肌酸能再生更多的 ATP。为了提高肌糖原的能量效率，运动员通过训练，一方面要避免无目的的糖原分解，另一方面要保证糖原在需要时的快速、大规模动员。

9.2.2 Exercise and the Glycogenesis in Muscle
运动与骨骼肌糖原合成

The effect of exercise on glycogenesis is indirect and much more complicated than the effect on glycogenolysis. The increased, decreased, and unchanged glycogen synthase activity during exercise has all been reported in the literature. Therefore, the net effect of exercise on glycogenesis in muscles depends on the relative strength of stimulatory and inhibitory signals, which may vary according to exercise parameters and muscle glycogen content.

During exercise, the using up of glycogen signals the activation of glycogen synthase. Short-term vigorous or maximum exercise seems to reduce glycogen synthase activity, while prolonged moderate-intensity exercise will increase it. After exercise, glycogen synthase remains activated for several hours to ensure rapid resynthesis of muscle glycogen.

与运动对糖原分解的影响相比，运动对糖原合成的影响更为间接和复杂。运动过程中糖原合酶活性的升高、降低和不变在文献中均有报道。因此，运动对肌肉中糖生成的净效应取决于刺激和抑制信号的相对强度，而这可能因运动类型、运动强度、运动持续时间等参数和肌糖原含量的不同而不同。

在运动中，糖原的消耗是糖原合酶激活的信号。短时间的极量或高强度运动似乎会降低糖原合酶活性，而长时间的中等强度运动则会提高糖原合酶活性。运动后，糖原合酶活性可保持活跃数小时，以确保肌糖原的快速重新合成。

9.2.3 Exercise and the Glycolysis in Muscle
运动与骨骼肌糖酵解

Exercise can accelerate the glycolysis rate in skeletal muscle by 100 times in multiple ways, such as increase of substrate availability, allosteric activation of phosphofructokinase, and regulation of pyruvate kinase (Figure 9.8).

Exercising muscles can increase their uptake of glucose from the blood by 50 times through increasing blood flow to the muscles as soon as the onset of muscle activity (up to 20 times the flow at rest), and augmenting the movement of glucose transporter 4 (GLUT 4) to the plasma membrane. The uptake of blood glucose by working muscles have a certain proportional relationship with exercise intensity and duration (Figure 9.9).

运动可以通过增加底物可用性、磷酸果糖激酶的变构激活和调节丙酮酸激酶等多种方式使骨骼肌中的糖酵解速率加快 100 倍（图 9.8）。

在运动开始后，机体可以通过增加骨骼肌的血流（比安静时增加 20 倍），增强葡萄糖转运体 4（GLUT 4）到质膜的运动，使骨骼肌从血液中摄取的葡萄糖增加 50 倍。运动肌对血糖的摄取与运动强度、运动持续时间成一定比例关系（图 9.9）。

The maximum rate of ATP resynthesis from glycogen to lactate in human muscles is estimated at $1.5 mmol/(kg \cdot s^{-1})$, and is reached within 5 s of maximal exercise. In contrast, the maximal rate of ATP re-synthesis from glycogen to CO_2 is estimated at $0.5 mmol/(kg \cdot s^{-1})$ and it requires more than 1 minute of maximum exercise to reach it. Therefore, anaerobic glycogen degradation becomes the major source for ATP resynthesis in the maximum exercise task lasting approximately 7 seconds to 1 minute. The maximum exercise task lasting more than 1 minute effect on glycogenolysis. The ... increased, decreased, and unchanged glycogen synthase activity during exercise has all been reported in the literature. Therefore, the net effect of exercise on glucose ... in muscle depends on the relative strength of stimulatory and inhibitory signals, which may vary according to exercise parameters and muscle glycogen content.

During exercise, the ... up in glycogen signals the activation of glycogen synthase. Short-term, vigorous or maximum exercise leads to reduced glycogen synthase activity, while prolonged moderate-intensity exercise will increase it. After exercise, glycogen synthase remains activated for several hours to ensure rapid resynthesis of muscle glycogen.

据 ... 肌糖原 ... 运动 ... 运动中 ... 运动强度 ... 最大运动或剧烈运动 ... 运动后糖原合成酶维持 ...

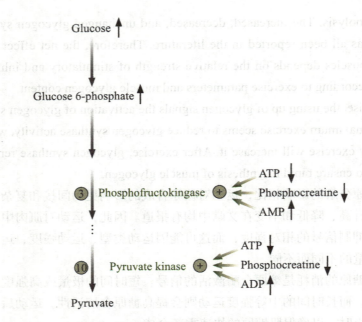

Figure 9.8   Control of glycolysis by exercise

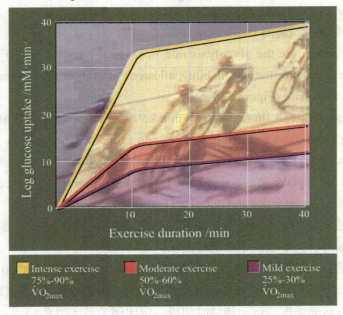

Figure 9.9   The uptake of blood glucose by the leg muscles during cycling

relies on aerobic glycogen degradation as its major energy source.

据估计，人体肌肉中糖原通过转化为乳酸再合成 ATP 的最大速率为 1.5 mmol/(kg·s⁻¹)，并在最大运动后 5 s 内达到。相比之下，糖原通过转化为 CO_2 再合成 ATP 的最大速率估计为 0.5mmol/(kg·s⁻¹)，需要超过 1 min 的最大运动才能达到。因此，糖原通过无氧代谢分解过程再合成的 ATP，成为持续约 7 s~1 min 的最大运动中 ATP 的主要来源；而糖原通过有氧代谢分解过程再合成的 ATP 成为超过 1 min 的最大运动中 ATP 的主要来源。

Because type II fibers do have higher contents of glycolytic enzymes and lactate dehydrogenase activity than type I fibers, type II fibers possess higher glycolytic power, and they synthesize ATP from glycolysis faster than type I fibers. Lactate formed during exercise can be taken up by the type I fibers and converted to pyruvate for further oxidization.

由于 II 型肌纤维比 I 型肌纤维具有更高的糖酵解酶含量和乳酸脱氢酶活性，因此 II 型纤维具有更高的糖酵解能力，并且通过糖酵解合成 ATP 的速度比 I 型肌纤维快。在运动过程中形成的乳酸可以被 I 型肌纤维吸收转化为丙酮酸，然后被氧化。

9.2.4 Exercise and the TCA cycle in Muscle
运动与骨骼肌三羧酸循环

Since the oxygen consumption increases with the increase in exercise intensity, the oxidation rate of acetyl group through the TCA cycle may increase as much as 100 times in the muscle during hard exercise. This increase is primarily due to the accelerated oxidation of pyruvate leading to an increase in acetyl CoA concentration. In addition, the cycle is accelerated during exercise by the allosteric regulation of citrate synthase, isocitrate dehydrogenase, and α-ketoglutarate dehydrogenase, which catalyze the first, fourth, and fifth reactions respectively (Figure 9.10).

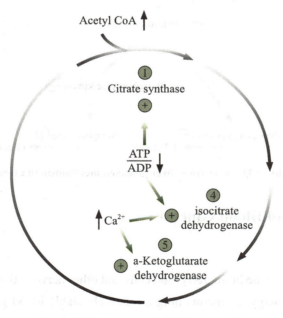

Figure 9.10   Control of TCA by exercise

由于运动中耗氧量随着运动强度的增加而增加，在剧烈的运动中，乙酰基通过三羧酸循环的氧化率可能会增加 100 倍，这种增加主要是由于丙酮酸氧化加速导致乙酰辅酶 A 浓度上升。此外，在运动过程中，分别催化第①、第④和第⑤步反应的柠檬酸合酶、异柠檬酸脱氢酶和 α - 酮戊二酸脱氢酶的变构调节加速了循环（图9.10）。

9.3 Exercise and Carbohydrate Metabolism in Liver
运动与肝脏的糖代谢

The main function of liver glycogen is to be converted into glucose and be secreted into bloodstream to provide energy for extrahepatic tissues. The level of liver glycogen is regulated by diet and exercise and varies widely. During exercise, the increased glucagon and epinephrine stimulates the cAMP cascade to speed up glycogenolysis and slow down glycogenesis in the liver (Figure 9.11).

肝糖原的主要作用是转化为葡萄糖并分泌到血液中，为肝外组织提供能量。肝糖原的含量受到饮食和运动的调控，变化很大。在运动过程中，胰高血糖素和肾上腺素的增加会通过刺激环腺苷酸（cAMP）级联反应加速肝糖原分解和减少肝糖原的合成。（图9.11）

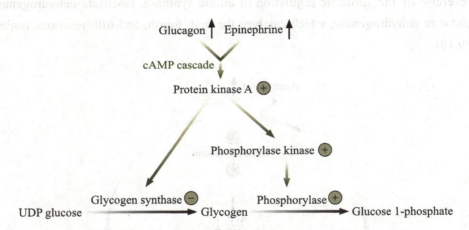

Figure 9.11　Control of liver glycogen metabolism in exercise

9.4 Exercise and Blood Glucose
运动与血糖

Some organs, such as the brain, red blood cells and other nervous tissues, almost use glucose as the only source of energy, so maintaining a relatively stable blood glucose concentration is vital for the normal functions of the whole body.

有些器官，如大脑、红细胞和其他神经组织等，几乎只使用葡萄糖作为供能物质，所以维持血糖水平的相对稳定对身体功能的正常发挥是至关重要的。

Exercise can cause significant fluctuations of blood glucose. For example, plasma glucose concentration can drop as low as 2.5 mmol/L after several hours of vigorous exercise. However, after a short period of vigorous exercise, plasma glucose concentration can exceed 10 mmol/L. Exercise can increase the formation and elimination rate of glucose in plasma. Thus, the plasma glucose concentration during exercise depends on the ratio of formation rate and elimination rate. In general, low intensity exercise does not significantly affect plasma glucose because it similarly augments the rate formation and elimination. Moderate or vigorous intensity exercise tends to increase plasma glucose in the initial stage and then decrease, because at the beginning of exercise, there is a higher hormonal stimulation for glucose release from the liver than its uptake by active muscles. As exercise continues, liver glycogen is gradually depleted, and plasma glucose even drops to the level at rest. Near extreme or maximum intensity and short-term exercise, which cannot be sustained for more than a few minutes, increases plasma glucose due to higher hepatic glycogen released than muscle uptaked.

运动可引起血糖水平的明显波动。例如，血糖浓度会在持续几个小时的力竭运动后降至 2.5mmol/L，但是在短时间的剧烈运动后，血糖浓度可超过 10mmol/L。运动增加了血浆中葡萄糖的出现率，也增加了葡萄糖的消失率，因此，运动期间的血糖浓度取决于葡萄糖的出现率和消失率的比值。一般来说，低强度运动对血糖影响不大，因为它对血糖的出现率和消失率的影响基本相似；中等到高强度运动往往会出现血糖浓度先升高后降低的现象。因为在运动初期，在激素的调控作用下，肝糖原的分解大于骨骼肌的葡萄糖摄取，随着运动时间延长，肝糖原逐渐耗尽，血糖甚至会低于安静水平。接近极量或最高强度的短时间（持续时间低于几分钟）运动，会增加血糖，同样是因为肝糖原的释放高于骨骼肌的吸收。

9.5 Exercise and Lactate
运动与乳酸

Strictly speaking, lactate is an anion formed when lactic acid dissociates. 99% of lactic acid is normally in its dissociated form.

严格地说，乳酸根是乳酸解离时形成的阴离子。99% 的乳酸是以游离的形式存在的。

$$Lactic\ acid \longleftrightarrow Lactat\text{-} + Hydrogen^+$$

$$(HLa \longleftrightarrow La\text{-} + H^+)$$

Because of cells, such as red blood cells, lack mitochondria and can only generate energy through anaerobic glycolysis, the human body constantly produces lactate. Because blood lactate is sensitive to exercise parameters, it has been a highly useful marker to evaluate the effects of exercise on metabolism. According to the exercise characteristics of the lactate curve, anaerobic metabolic capacity and aerobic endurance can be estimated, and a training plan can be drafted.

由于红细胞等细胞缺乏线粒体，只能通过无氧糖酵解产生能量，因此人体会不断地产生乳酸。由于血乳酸对运动参数很敏感，因此它已成为运动对代谢影响的一个非常有用的指标。根据运动中乳酸变化曲线的特点，可以评估运动员的无氧代谢能力和有氧耐力，评价训练计划。

9.5.1 Exercise and the Lactate Metabolism in Muscle
运动与骨骼肌乳酸代谢

Normally, the production and removal of lactate maintain a balance. During exercise, skeletal muscle is the major producer of lactate. Lactate can be eliminated in many ways, including oxidation to carbon dioxide and water through the TCA cycle, or the conversion to glucose (in the liver, but not in muscle) or glycogen (in the liver and/or muscle) through gluconeogenesis and so on.

During exercise, lactate produced in skeletal muscle is shuttled out of the muscle cells and transported to the liver through the blood. In the liver, lactate contributes to glucose production. The glucose produced from lactate is subsequently released back into the bloodstream, transported back to the exercising skeletal muscle and used as fuel. This lactate-to-glucose cycle between skeletal muscle and liver is known as the Cori cycle (Figure 9.12) and it represents an effective way to prevent the accumulation of blood lactate.

正常情况下，乳酸的产生和消除保持平衡。运动过程中，骨骼肌是乳酸的主要生产者。而乳酸的消除途径有很多种，包括通过三羧酸循环氧化成二氧化碳和水；通过糖异生转化为葡萄糖（在肝脏中，但不在肌肉中）或糖原（在肝脏和 / 或肌肉中）等。

在运动过程中，骨骼肌产生的乳酸从肌细胞中穿梭出来，通过血液运送到肝脏。在肝脏内，乳酸异生成葡萄糖并被释放入血，再经过血液循环运送到运动中的骨骼肌，作为燃料。骨骼肌和肝脏之间的乳酸 – 葡萄糖循环被称为 Cori 循环（图 9.12），是一种防止血乳酸积累的有效方法。

It had been suggested that lactate production in muscles impaired function of muscle contract and led to acidosis. But biochemical evidence reveals that during intense exercise, muscles must produce lactate to regenerate cytosolic NAD^+ and maintain a high ATP turnover rate produced by glycolysis. In other words, muscles need to produce lactate to sustain repeated intense muscle contractions. The H^+ formation and the drop in cytosolic pH should be accepted as the result of the entire process of anaerobic carbohydrate degradation. Lactate is only the end product of this process. Therefore, the traditional interpretation of acidosis is incorrect. Lactate production may not be the cause of fatigue that we have always thought.

以往的观点认为肌乳酸产生会引起酸中毒，进而使骨骼肌的收缩功能受损。但生物化学证据显示，在剧烈运动中，肌肉中乳酸的生成是细胞内 NAD^+ 再生的必要条件，此过程有利于维持糖酵解过程中 ATP 的高速周转。换句话说，肌肉需要乳酸来维持反复剧烈的肌肉收缩。H^+ 的形成和细胞质 pH 值的下降应该被看作是糖的整个无氧分解过程的结果，乳酸只是这个过程的最终产物，因此传统的酸中毒解释是不正确的。乳酸的产生可能不是我们一直认为的疲劳的原因。

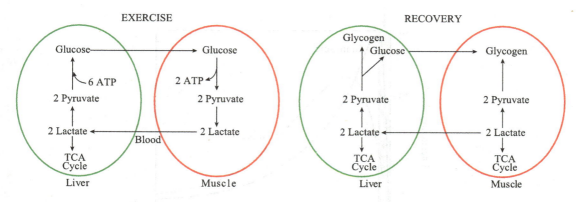

Figure 9.12   Regulation of Cori cycle by exercise

9.5.2 Exercise and Blood Lactate
运动与血乳酸

During exercise, blood lactate response not only depends on the intensity, duration, and program of the exercise, but also on gender, age, nutritional status and environmental factors.

在运动过程中，血乳酸反应不仅与运动强度、持续时间和运动计划有关，还与性别、年龄、营养状况和一些环境因素有关。

9.5.2.1 Exercise Time and Blood Lactate
运动时间与血乳酸

During the rest period, the steady state of blood lactate concentration is approximately 1 mmol/L. When we begin exercising, lactate that mainly comes from active muscle begins to accumulate in blood, which can be measured as early as one minute after the onset of strenuous exercise. If we continue to exercise at a steady pace, the accumulation of blood lactate diminishes gradually. Usually, 2~10 min after the onset of exercise, blood lactate concentration reaches its maximum. At the end of exercise, the lactate concentration in the exercising muscle arrives at the peak, and is higher than blood. When we stop exercising, muscle lactate concentration begins to decrease, then the blood lactate concentration also decreases in the next few minutes (Figure 9.13).

安静状态下，血乳酸浓度相对稳定地保持在 1 mmol/L 左右。当我们开始运动时，主要来自骨骼肌的乳酸开始在血液中积累，在剧烈运动开始 1 min 后就可以检测出来。如果我们继续以稳定的速度运动，血乳酸的积累就会逐渐减少。通常在开始运动 2 ~ 10 min 后，血乳酸浓度达到最大值。在运动结束时，运动肌中的乳酸浓度达到峰值，高于血液中的乳酸浓度。停止运动后，肌乳酸浓度开始下降，几分钟后，血乳酸浓度也随之变化（图 9.13）。

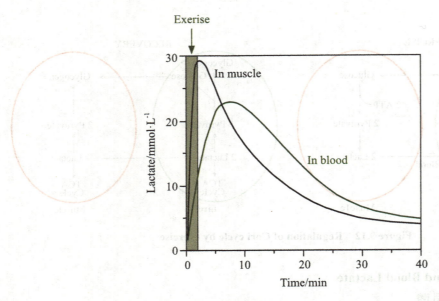

Figure 9.13 Lactate-time curve

9.5.2.2 Exercise Intensity and Blood Lactate
运动强度与血乳酸

Low-intensity exercise will not cause a significant increase of blood lactate, because carbohydrates are mainly broken down aerobically. During prolonged constant moderate-intensity exercise, as the energy contribution from carbohydrates decreases, blood lactate also decreases. After one and a half minute vigorous exercise, the blood lactate level can increase significantly, but less than 20mmol/L. However, the maximum intensity exercise that lasts more than one and a half minutes will result in a lactate concentration increasing more than 20mmol/L. If the intensity fluctuates, as in ball games and interval training, the lactate concentration will fluctuate between the values corresponding to the highest and lowest intensities.

Through the incremental load experiment, we can get the curve of lactate concentration versus exercise intensity (Figure 9.14). The blood lactate concentration increases exponentially with the increase of exercise intensity. Lactate threshold, also known as anaerobic threshold, is defined as the exercise intensity above which blood lactate begins to rise rapidly, or the exercise intensity corresponding to a blood lactate concentration of 4 mmol/L. The lactate threshold is often considered to be the transition point from aerobic to anaerobic catabolism for energy production. But such a thing does not really exist. There is no state of exclusively aerobic or exclusively anaerobic metabolism during exercise and even in the rest state. Therefore, some exercise scientists and coaches tend to name it as "an intensity corresponding to a blood lactate concentration of 4 mmol/L".

　　由于糖类在低强度的运动中主要是通过有氧代谢来分解的，因此低强度运动不会导致血乳酸的显著增加。在长时间持续的中等强度运动中，血乳酸随着糖类供能比例的下降而逐渐下降。持续时间不超过 1.5 min 的最高强度运动可以产生较高的乳酸浓度，但低于 20 mmol/L；然而，持续时间超过 1.5 min 的最高强度运动可以产生超过 20 mmol/L 的乳酸浓度。如果强度是波动的，就像球类运动和间歇训练，那么乳酸浓度就在对应的最高和最低强度值之间。

　　通过递增负荷实验，我们可以得到乳酸浓度与运动强度的关系曲线（图 9.14）。血乳酸浓度随运动强度的增加而呈指数级增加。乳酸阈强度，又称无氧阈强度，是指血液中的乳酸浓度开始快速升高的运动强度，或血乳酸浓度为 4 mmol/L 时所对应的运动强度。乳酸阈值通常被认为是机体从有氧代谢供能过渡到无氧代谢供能的转折点。但这种情况实际并不存在，在运动过程中，甚至在休息状态中，都不存在完全有氧代谢或完全无氧代谢的状态。因此，一些运动科学专家和教练员倾向于将其命名为"与血乳酸浓度 4 mmol/L 相对应的强度"。

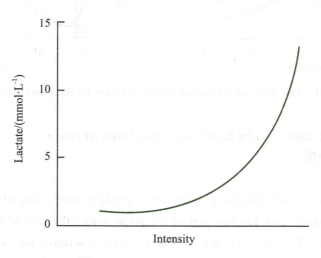

图 9.14 **Lactate-Intensity curve**

9.5.2.3 Exercise and Blood Lactate Removal
运动与血乳酸的消除

The half-life of blood lactate is at least 12 min. In order to accelerate the removal of lactate, athletes are often encouraged to perform some active recovery (continue to exercise at about 20%–40% of their $\dot{V}O_2max$) after strenuous or maximum exercise, rather than rest (passive recovery). Research has shown that active recovery can speed up the return of blood lactate and pH to baseline levels (Figure 9.15). However, there is no consensus on whether active recovery will accelerate the disappearance of active muscle lactate or the restoration of resting muscle pH, and whether these effects provide any benefit for subsequent exercise.

血乳酸的半衰期至少是 12 min。为了加快乳酸的去除，在极量或高强度运动后，运动员经常被鼓励做一些积极性的主动恢复（继续以 20%~40% 的最大摄氧量进行运动），而不是休息（被动恢复）。研究表明，主动恢复可以加速血乳酸和 pH 值恢复到基线水平（图9.15）。但对于积极性的主动恢复是否会加速肌乳酸的消失或恢复静息肌肉 pH 值，目前尚无一致结论；骨骼肌中乳酸和 pH 值的恢复是否有利于随后的运动，也尚不清楚。

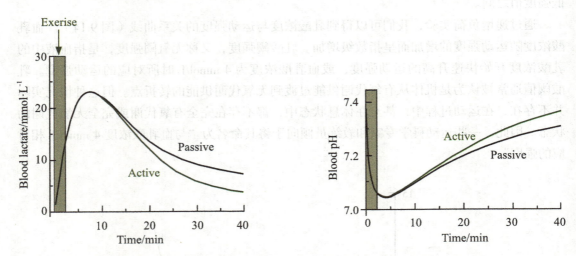

Figure 9.15   The effects of active and passive recovery on the blood lactate and pH

9.6 Exercise and Carbohydrate Supplementation
运动与补糖

Moderate or vigorous intensity exercise exceeding one hour, either continuous or intermittent, can reduce muscle glycogen to the point where the rate of ATP regeneration is reduced substantially (Figure 9.16), and aerobic endurance performance is affected. But these adverse effects can be ameliorated by proper intake of carbohydrates before, during and after exercise.

Before exercise, an excessive high-carbohydrate intake for several days in a row has been termed carbohydrate loading. A successful carbohydrate loading requires a careful combination of dieting and training. A typical protocol may begin six days before the event with moderate carbohydrate intake (providing 40%–50% of daily energy) and regular training for three days. Such combination aims to lower muscle glycogen content to active glycogen synthase. Then, in the final three days before the event, the carbohydrate intake is increased to about 70% of daily energy intake in order to provide ample substrate for the upregulated muscle glycogen synthase. In addition, training load is tapered off to curb glycogen breakdown. But some studies have reported that carbohydrate loading can only double the muscle and liver glycogen contents of men, and improve performance in events that lasted more than 90 min.

During exercise, carbohydrates supplementation can result in a spectacular rise in its contribution to ATP resynthesis and maintaining euglycemia, so as to improve exercise performance. The amount and type of carbohydrate supplementation are related to the intensity and duration of exercise. Cycling at 70%–75% $\dot{V}O_2$max, without carbohydrate supplement, experienced athletes are exhausted after approximately 3 h, and the contribution of carbohydrates to whole body energy production has fallen below 30%(Figure 9.17 a). With carbohydrates supplement, athletes can ride for an additional hour, and carbohydrates still contribute half of the total energy in the end (Figure 9.17 b). Usually, moderate or low-intensity exercise under 60 min does not need carbohydrates supplementation. If the exercise duration is 60 min to 2 h, 30 g/h carbohydrates supplementation should be given in the form of either single or multiple carbohydrates. The longer exercise duration, the more carbohydrates supplement you will need. If the exercise duration is more than 3 h, 90 g/h carbohydrates should be supplemented using multiple carbohydrates (Figure 9.18).

持续时间超过 1 h 的中等强度或高强度运动，无论是连续运动还是间歇运动，都可以减少肌糖原储量，从而使 ATP 再生速度大幅下降（图 9.16），并影响有氧耐力。但是这种不利的影响可以通过在运动前、运动中和运动后适量地补充糖类而得到改善。

运动前，连续几天摄入大量高糖膳食称为糖负荷。成功的糖负荷需要饮食控制与运动训练的谨慎结合。一项典型的方案是在比赛前 6 天开始适量摄入糖类食物，使糖类提供的能量占每日能量的 40%~50%，同时进行 3 天的常规训练。这种结合的目的是降低骨骼肌糖原含量，以诱导糖原合酶。然后，在比赛前的最后 3 天，糖类的摄入量增加到占每日能量的 70%，以便为上调的肌糖原合酶提供充足的底物。此外，训练负荷逐渐减小，以抑制糖原分解。但有研究报道，糖负荷只能使男性的肌肉和肝脏糖原含量增加一倍，并提高 90 min 以上运动的运动表现。

运动中补糖有助于提高糖类在 ATP 重新合成中的贡献及维持正常血糖，进而提高运动表现。运动中补糖的数量及种类与运动持续时间和运动强度有关。在长时间的中等或大强度运动中，在不补充糖的情况下，有经验的自行车运动员以 70%~75% 最大摄氧量强度的速度骑行约 3 h 后就筋疲力尽，其中糖类对全身能量的贡献率下降到 30% 以下（图 9.17 a）；通过补充糖类，运动员可以额外运动 1 h，且在运动结束时糖类的供能仍然可以达到总能量的一半（图 9.17 b）。通常在 60 min 以下的中、低强度运动不需要补糖，60 min 到 2 h 的运动可以以 30 g/h 的补充量来补充一种糖或多种糖。随着持续运动时间延长，补糖量逐渐增加，如果持续运动时间在 3 h 以上，补糖量可以达到 90 g/h（图 9.18）。

During exercise, athletes can obtain carbohydrates in a variety of ways, such as sports drinks, gels and energy bars. Sports drinks usually contain 6%–8% of carbohydrates and provide optimal hydration as well as energy. The available evidence shows that the most effective approach to maximize absorption of both carbohydrate and fluid is to ingest a mixture of multiple

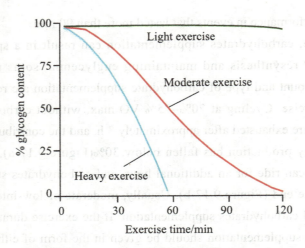

Figure 9.16   Carbohydrate utilization in exercise

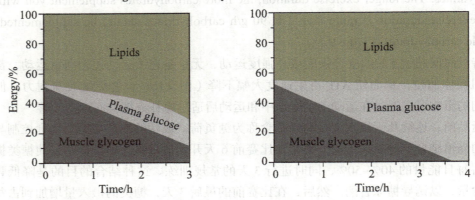

Figure 9.17   Carbohydrate supplementation during exercise

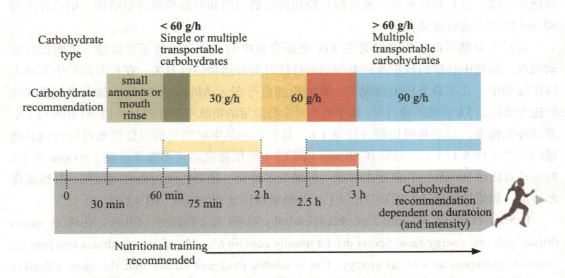

Figure 9.18   The recommendation of carbohydrate intake during exercise

types of carbohydrate involving both active and passive transport mechanisms. A proper carbohydrate concentration can be selected by considering its oxidation rate in muscles during exercise and its absorption rate in small intestine together with the osmotic pressure of ingested solution.

Supplementing carbohydrates after exercise helps to promote the recovery of the body. Because in the post-exercise recovery process, muscle ATP is resynthesized from ADP through oxidative phosphorylation in the mitochondria, and it is mainly fueled by the combustion of carbohydrates. Sufficient carbohydrates are also required to supplement muscle and liver glycogen stores. The rate of glycogen recovery is the fastest in the first 0–5 h or 0–10 h after short-term high-intensity exercise or endurance exercise, and will be able to continue for 24 h or 48 h. To speed up the glycogen recovery, carbohydrate supplementation should be started immediately after exercise. If we consume sufficient carbohydrates after exercise, insulin secretion will be improved, insulin sensitivity will be increased and glycogenesis will be promoted.

在运动过程中，运动员可以通过多种方式补充糖，例如，运动饮料、凝胶和能量棒等。运动饮料通常含有 6%~8% 的糖，可以在提供能量的同时，实现最佳的水合作用。有证据表明，实现最大吸收量的补液有效策略，应兼顾糖的主动运输和被动运输，而选择由多种类型的糖组成的混合糖。选择适宜的糖浓度时，应综合考虑运动时糖类在肌肉中的氧化速率、在小肠中的吸收率以及所摄入溶液的渗透压。

运动后补糖有利于促进机体的恢复。因为在运动后的恢复过程中，骨骼肌中的 ATP 是由线粒体中的 ADP 经氧化磷酸化再合成的，而 ATP 再合成主要靠糖类的燃烧提供能量。同时，肌糖原和肝糖原储量的恢复也需要足够的糖类。在短时间大强度运动后 0~5 h，或耐力运动后 0~10 h，糖原恢复最快，并可分别持续 24 h 或 48 h。因此，为了加速糖原恢复，运动后即刻就应该补糖。如果能在运动后摄入足够的糖，可引起胰岛素分泌增加，胰岛素敏感性增强，促进糖原合成。

Chapter 10　Lipid Metabolism in Exercise

第十章　运动与脂代谢

Fat is the largest energy depot in the body and exhibits the highest variability among individuals. Athletes usually have lower body fat content compared with non-athletes with the same gender, age, and body mass index (BMI).

脂肪是人体最大的能量库，个体之间的差异最大。运动员的体脂含量通常低于同性别、同年龄、同体重指数（BMI）的非运动员。

10.1 Lipid Metabolism
脂代谢

10.1.1 Lipolysis
脂肪分解

Lipolysis is a process of which triglycerides (TAGs) are broken down into glycerol and fatty acids by the sequential action of three enzymes: adipose triacylglycerol lipase (ATGL), hormone-sensitive lipase (HSL) and monoacylglycerol lipase (MGL) (Figure 10.1). Lipolysis takes place in adipose tissue and muscles, and is regulated by hormones such as epinephrine and insulin.

Depending on food intake and physical activity level, lipolysis can break down about 100–300 g of triacylglycerols in the body each day. Normally, Lipolysis does not occur within 1–2 h after a meal, particularly if the meal is high in carbohydrates. Lipolysis gradually increases around 6 h or more after a meal, and also during exercise when fatty acids are needed as an energy source by various tissues.

脂肪（甘油三酯，TAGs）分解是通过三种酶——脂肪三酰基甘油脂肪酶（ATGL）、激素敏感脂肪酶（HSL）和单酰基甘油酯酶（MGL）的依次作用，将甘油三酯分解为甘油和脂肪酸的过程（图 10.1）。脂肪分解发生在脂肪和肌肉组织中，受肾上腺素和胰岛素等激素的调节。

受食物摄入量及身体活动水平的影响，人体每天可通过脂解作用分解 100~300 g 的脂肪。一般情况下，脂肪分解不会在餐后 1~2 h 内发生，尤其是在食物中糖类含量较高的情况下。在餐后 6 h 及以后，脂肪分解发生逐渐增加，运动中也有脂肪分解，此时脂肪酸是各种组织的能量来源。

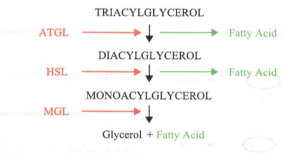

Figure 10.1   Lipolysis

10.1.2 Fatty Acid Oxidation
脂肪酸氧化

Lipolysis takes place in the cytosol of adipocyte, while further degradation of fatty acids occurs in the mitochondria. Therefore, the fatty acids in the cytosol will be activated by fatty acyl CoA synthetase (ACS), and then carried by L-carnitine as the acyl CoA to the mitochondria.

β-oxidation is the pathway of fatty acids degradation in the mitochondria. Acyl CoA undergoes the four reactions of β-oxidation and ends in the detachment of two carbons, in the form of acetyl CoA, from the carboxyl end of the acyl group (Figure 10.2). The process of β-oxidation is repeated as many times as the fatty acid fully degrade into the acetyl CoA, and then enters the TCA cycle.

There is a great amount of energy arising from fatty acid oxidation, which is more than glucose oxidation. But fatty acids are only used in aerobic activities because the TCA cycle and oxidative phosphorylation are involved.

脂肪分解发生在脂肪细胞的细胞质中，而脂肪酸的进一步降解发生在线粒体中。因此，细胞质中的脂肪酸要被脂酰辅酶 A 合成酶（ACS）激活，然后以脂酰辅酶 A 的形式被 L-肉碱带入线粒体。

β-氧化是脂肪酸在线粒体中降解的途径。脂酰辅酶 A 经过一次 β-氧化的 4 步反应，以乙酰辅酶 A 的形式从碳链的羧基端分离两个碳（图 10.2）。经过 β-氧化的多次重复，脂肪酸完全降解为乙酰辅酶 A，然后进入三羧酸循环。

　　脂肪酸氧化产生的能量远远大于葡萄糖氧化产生的能量，但脂肪酸的氧化只在有三羧酸循环和氧化磷酸化的有氧代谢中才发生。

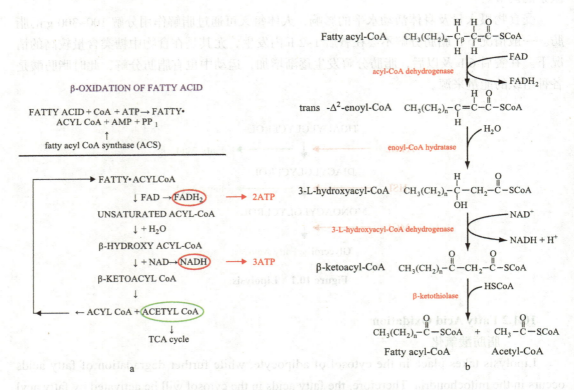

Figure 10.2　β-oxidation of fatty acids

10.1.3 Ketone Body
酮体

Because of insufficient oxaloacetate, acetyl CoA can not be finally oxidized to CO_2 in the liver, so two acetyl CoA combined to form a ketone body (a collective term for acetoacetate, 3-hydroxybutyrate and acetone). The production of ketone body increases the availability of fat.

Ketone bodies exit from the mitochondria of hepatocytes and diffuse into the blood. Acetone is usually exhaled from the lungs, while acetoacetate and 3-hydroxybutyrate are taken up by extrahepatic tissues, including heart, kidneys, brain, and skeletal muscle. They are reconverted into acetyl-CoA and acetyl-CoA thereafter enters the TCA cycle for oxidation. Thus, ketone bodies can be used as fuel by extrahepatic tissues (Figure 10.3).

　　由于草酰乙酸不足，乙酰辅酶 A 在肝脏中最终不能氧化为 CO_2，所以两个乙酰辅酶 A 会结合在一起形成酮体（乙酰乙酸、3– 羟基丁酸和丙酮的总称）。酮体的生成增加了脂肪的可用性。

酮体离开肝细胞的线粒体，扩散到血液中。丙酮通常从肺呼出体外，而乙酰乙酸和 3-羟基丁酸则被肝外组织，如心脏、肾脏、大脑、骨骼肌吸收利用。在这些组织中，乙酰乙酸和 3- 羟基丁酸被重新转化为乙酰辅酶 A，再进入三羧酸循环进行氧化。因此，酮体可以作为肝外组织燃料被利用（图 10.3）。

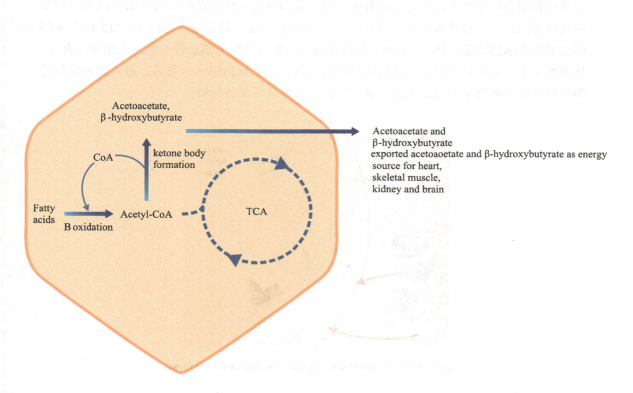

Figure 10.3   Reuse of Ketone body; acetoacetate, D-3-hydroxybutyrate and acetone

10.1.4 Triacylglycerol synthesis
脂肪合成

The essence of triacylglycerol synthesis is the reverse process of lipolysis. Triacylglycerols are made from three acyl CoAs and L-glycerol-3-phosphate. Figure 10.4 highlights the use of glucose to produce the glycerol backbone of the triacylglycerol, and the fatty acids which are attached to the glycerol backbone. Both glucose and fatty acids may come from the diet or be synthesized by the liver. Glucose enters adipocytes to produce the glycerol-phosphate, which is regulated by insulin. Insulin enhances the translocation of GLUT4 from intracellular vesicles to the plasma membrane, just as what it does in muscle fibers. In addition, insulin will increase the content of lipoprotein lipase in the capillaries of adipose tissue, thereby enhancing the hydrolysis of triacylglycerols in chylomicrons and the delivery of fatty acids to adipocytes. After a meal, the amounts of glucose and fatty acids that enter the adipocytes are increased, causing the synthesis of triacylglycerol to outweigh the breakdown in the postprandial state.

脂肪合成的实质是脂解作用的逆过程。脂肪由 3 个脂酰辅酶 A 和 L–3– 磷酸 – 甘油合成。如图 10.4 所示，葡萄糖提供了脂肪合成的磷酸甘油，随后脂肪酸连接在甘油主链上。葡萄糖和脂肪酸可能来自饮食或由肝脏合成。葡萄糖进入脂肪细胞形成磷酸甘油的过程受到胰岛素的调节。就像在肌肉纤维中一样，胰岛素增强了葡萄糖转运体 4（GLUT4）从脂肪细胞内囊泡到质膜的转运。此外，胰岛素增加了脂肪组织毛细血管中脂蛋白脂酶的含量，从而增强了乳糜微粒中脂肪的水解以及脂肪酸向脂肪细胞的输送。餐后，进入脂肪细胞的葡萄糖和脂肪酸数量增加，因此餐后的脂肪合成超过了脂肪分解。

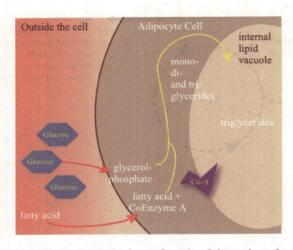

Figure 10.4　General schema for triacylglycerol synthesis

10.2 Exercise and Lipid Metabolism
　　运动与脂代谢

10.2.1 Exercise and Lipolysis
　　运动与脂肪分解

Studies have shown that within 5–10 minutes after the onset of exercise, the lipase activity in adipose tissue is the highest, and the amount of lipolytic products excreted from adipocytes is increased. Exercise primarily speeds up lipolysis in adipose tissue by increasing the release of epinephrine into the bloodstream. Epinephrine, which binds to the β-adrenergic receptors located in the plasma membrane of adipocytes, stimulates the cAMP cascade and activates lipolysis. Insulin inhibits the lipolytic action of epinephrine. As we know, insulin secretion usually decreases during moderate-intensity exercise, which favors lipolysis over triacylglycerol synthesis. During hard or maximum exercise, the influence of insulin on the balance between lipolysis and triacylglycerol synthesis becomes small.

研究表明，在运动开始的 5~10 min，脂肪组织中脂肪酶活性最大，来自脂肪细胞的脂质分解产物生成增加。运动主要是通过促进肾上腺素释放入血，加速脂肪组织的脂肪分解。肾上腺素与位于脂肪细胞膜上的肾上腺素能受体结合，刺激 cAMP 级联反应，激活脂解作用。胰岛素与肾上腺素的作用相反。我们知道，在中等强度的运动中，胰岛素分泌通常会减少，这有利于脂肪分解，但不利于脂肪合成。在高强度或极量运动中，胰岛素对脂肪分解和合成之间的平衡的影响变得很小。

The lipolysis in muscle can also be accelerated by exercise. But compared with adipocytes, we know little about the control of lipolysis in muscle fibers.

运动也可以加速肌肉内的脂肪分解，但与脂肪细胞相比，我们对肌肉纤维中脂肪分解的调控了解得很少。

Plasma triacylglycerols basically do not participate in energy supply during exercise. However, the acceleration of lipolysis during exercise leads to an increase in the appearance of fatty acids and glycerol in the plasma. Glycerol is soluble. Plasma glycerol can be taken up by the liver or muscle and be used for gluconeogenesis or glycolysis. Although the fatty acids are poorly soluble, they are carried by albumin in the blood and absorbed by the liver for triacylglycerol synthesis, or by muscles for ATP regeneration (Figure 10.5). Therefore, the amount of fatty acids delivered from adipose tissue to muscle is dependent on the blood flow through the adipose tissue and the number of albumin molecules in the blood. The number of fatty acid transporters can be up-regulated in endurance-trained athletes. They can utilize more fatty acids as energy sources.

在运动过程中，血浆中的甘油三酯不参与能量供应，但是运动过程中脂肪分解的加速会导致血浆中脂肪酸和甘油的含量增加。甘油具有可溶性，血浆中的甘油可被肝脏或肌肉吸收，用于糖异生或糖酵解。虽然脂肪酸溶解性差，但可以以与白蛋白结合的形式在血液中运输，经肝脏吸收用于三酰甘油合成，或经肌肉吸收用于 ATP 再生（图 10.5）。因此，脂肪酸从脂肪组织输送到肌肉的数量取决于通过脂肪组织的血液流量和血液中白蛋白分子的数量。经过耐力训练的运动员可以调节脂肪酸转运体的数量，因此可以吸收和利用更多的脂肪酸作为供能物质。

10.2.2 Exercise and Fatty Acid Oxidation
运动与脂肪酸氧化

Although fatty acid oxidation produces more energy than glucose oxidation, the maximum rate of ATP resynthesis through the oxidation of fatty acids from muscle [0.3 mmol/(kg · s^{-1})] and adipose tissue [0.2 mmol/(kg · s^{-1})] are lower than the maximal rate of ATP resynthesis through carbohydrate oxidation [0.5 mmol/(kg · s^{-1})]. Therefore, fatty acid cannot fully support strenuous exercise. In contrast, fatty acid is the major energy source at rest and during light exercise (Figure 10.6).

　　虽然从脂肪酸氧化产生的能量比葡萄糖氧化多，但是肌肉和脂肪组织中脂肪酸氧化再合成 ATP 的最大速率分别为 0.3 mmol/(kg·s⁻¹)、0.2 mmol/(kg·s⁻¹)，低于糖类氧化再合成的 ATP 最大速率 [0.5 mmol/(kg·s⁻¹)]。因此，脂肪酸不能支持高强度运动。相比之下，脂肪酸是休息和低强度运动时的主要供能物质（图 10.6）。

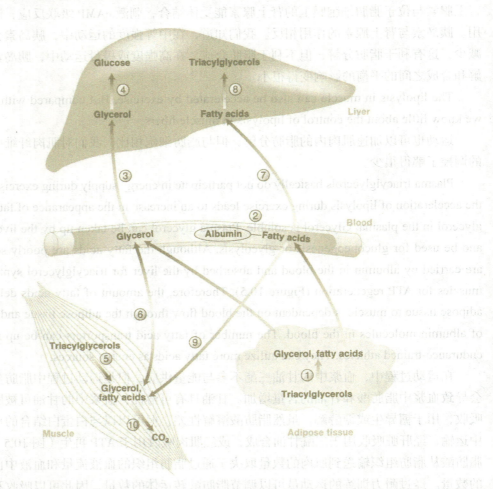

Figure 10.5　**The metabolism of lipolytic products during exercise. Triacylglycerols in adipose tissue are broken down to fatty acids and glycerol ①, which are released to the bloodstream and taken up by other tissues. Fatty acids bind to albumin for transport in the blood ②. Glycerol enters the liver ③, and the liver uses it to make glucose ④. In muscle, triacylglycerols are broken down into glycerol and fatty acids ⑤. Glycerol can also enter muscles ⑥. Blood-borne fatty acids can either enter the liver ⑦, where the liver uses them to produce triacylglycerols ⑧, or enter the muscles ⑨, where they join the local fatty acids and are oxidized to CO_2 ⑩**

　　As shown in Figure 10.6, during low-intensity exercise, demand for fatty acids in muscle is low and lipolytic rate in adipose tissue is high, thus the plasma fatty acid concentration rises. In moderate-intensity exercise, plasma fatty acids decrease first and then increase. Because in the early stages of exercise, fatty acid degradation increases faster than the hormonal stimulation of lipolysis. However, as lipolysis catches up with fatty acid degradation, the concentration of fatty acids in blood rises and can exceed 2 mmol/L during very prolonged exercise tasks. Compared with untrained people, trained individuals have a slightly lower increase during moderate-intensity exercise. Finally, the plasma fatty acid concentration keep below the baseline during vigorous exercise. The main reason for this drop is vasoconstriction, which induces a decrease in the blood flow to adipose tissue, thereby decreasing the movement of fatty acids. After the exercise, the plasma concentration of fatty acids rises rapidly because their utilization in the muscles almost decreases instantaneously, whereas it takes a few minutes for the hormones to inhibit lipolysis. In addition, the blood flow to the adipose tissue returns to normal by vasodilation, which allows the fatty acids trapped in the interstitial fluid to release into the bloodstream.

如图 10.6 所示，在低强度运动中，由于肌肉对脂肪酸的需求量低，脂肪组织中脂肪分解率高，所以血浆脂肪酸浓度升高；中等强度运动时，血浆脂肪酸表现为先下降后升高的特点。因为在运动初期，脂肪酸分解的增加比激素调控的脂肪分解作用要快。运动中，随着脂肪分解速度的加快，脂肪酸浓度上升。在超长时间的运动中，血浆脂肪酸浓度可超过 2 mmol/L。在中等强度的运动中，受过训练的个体与未受过训练的个体相比，血浆脂肪酸浓度增加的幅度略低；在高强度运动中，血浆脂肪酸浓度始终低于基线水平。导致脂肪酸含量下降的主要原因是血管收缩。血管收缩导致流向脂肪组织的血液减少，从而减少了脂肪酸的输送。运动结束后，血浆中脂肪酸的浓度就会快速上升，因为肌肉会立刻停止消耗脂肪酸，而激素调控的脂解作用的停止则需要几分钟。此外，通过血管扩张，脂肪组织的血流恢复正常，这使得之前被困在组织间液中的脂肪酸进入血液。

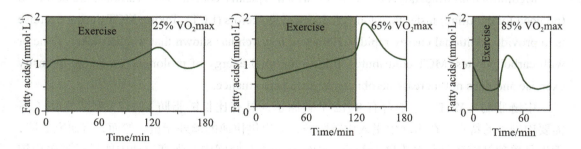

Figure 10.6　Plasma fatty acid concentration during exercise of different intensity

10.2.3 Exercise and Ketone Body Metabolism
运动与酮体代谢

Exercise can speed up the metabolism of ketone bodies. It is reported that the concentration of ketone bodies in blood and the ketolytic rate in muscles increased during prolonged exercise, although neither of them has been high enough to render acetoacetate and 3-hydroxybutyrate as the major fuels for the active muscles. The contribution of ketone bodies to energy expenditure during exercise ranges from 2%–10%.

运动可以加快酮体的新陈代谢。据报道，血液中的酮体浓度和肌肉中的酮体分解速率在长时间的运动中增加，但是没有高到足以使乙酰乙酸和 3- 羟基丁酸成为运动肌肉的主要燃料。在运动过程中，酮体对能量消耗的贡献为 2%~10%。

10.3 Exercise and Fat Supplementation 运动与脂肪补充

Low-carbohydrate high-fat diet (ketogenic diet) consists in obtaining 60%–80% of daily energy from fat for one or more weeks, thereby forcing the body to use fats as the main energy source instead of carbohydrates. Body adaptations include increased myocellular triacylglycerols, increased uptake of plasma fatty acids by active muscles, and more plasma triacylglycerols are used to produce energy. But when endurance athletes were training on a low-carbohydrate high-fat diet for three weeks, their performance did not improve, while it did improve among athletes on a high-carbohydrate diet.

低糖高脂饮食（生酮饮食）是指每天从脂肪中获得 60%~80% 的能量，持续一个或多个星期，从而迫使机体燃烧脂肪而不是糖类。机体的适应性变化包括肌细胞中脂肪含量增加，运动肌对血浆脂肪酸的吸收增加，以及利用血浆甘油三酯产生能量。但当耐力运动员在三周的训练中同时摄入低糖高脂食物时，他们的运动表现并没有改善，而摄入高糖食物的运动员的运动表现却有所改善。

Medium-chain triacylglycerols (MCT), which typically contain 8–12 carbons, are absorbed (no need for carnitine) faster than long-chain triacylglycerols (LCT). Taking MCT during exercise is to provide additional energy rapidly. However, research has shown that whether taken alone or with carbohydrates, MCT contributes little to the total energy of prolonged moderate-intensity exercise and does not increase aerobic endurance performance.

中链脂肪（MCT）通常含有 8~12 个碳原子，具有比长链脂肪（LCT）吸收更快（不需要肉碱）的特点。在运动中摄入中链脂肪，以提供快速的额外能量。然而，有研究表明，无论是单独补充还是与糖类联合补充，中链脂肪在长时间中等强度运动中能量贡献率均较小，不足以提高有氧耐力水平。

Chapter 11　Protein Metabolism in Exercise

第十一章　运动与蛋白质代谢

Proteins play a pivotal role in life as enzymes, transporters, receptors, peptide hormones and so on. There is no excess protein in the body to make up for possible deficiencies, so the survival, health, and performance of the organism depend heavily on the integrity of its proteins.

蛋白质作为酶、转运体、受体、肽类激素等在生命的各种功能中起着举足轻重的作用。人体中没有储存多余的蛋白质来弥补可能的蛋白质短缺，因此有机体的生存、健康和机能在很大程度上依赖于其蛋白质的完整性。

11.1 Protein Metabolism
蛋白质代谢

11.1.1 Protein Balance
蛋白质平衡

The synthesis and breakdown of protein follow different metabolic pathways. Protein synthesis is more complex because it first requires precise transcription of DNA information into mRNA, and then needs precise translation of the information into amino acid sequence. Protein breakdown is catalyzed by proteases (Figure 11.1).

蛋白质的合成和分解遵循不同的代谢途径。蛋白质的合成更为复杂，因为它首先需要将 DNA 的信息精确地转录到信使核糖核酸（mRNA）上，然后再精确地翻译成氨基酸序列。蛋白质的分解由蛋白酶催化（图 11.1）。

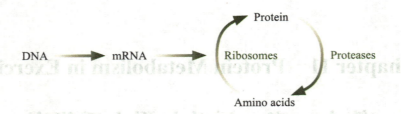

Figure 11.1   The synthesis and breakdown of protein

11.1.2 Amino Acid Catabolism
氨基酸分解代谢

Amino acids, the products of proteolysis, can be broken down to produce energy through their respective catabolic pathways. The 21 amino acids, which are the building blocks of proteins, are first discarded of their α-amino group by deamination, transamination, oxidative deamination and non-oxidative deamination. Then they enter pathways of carbohydrate and lipid metabolism, where they are catabolized aerobically to CO_2 and yield ATP (Figure 11.2).

Amino acids either in whole (Ala, Cys, Gly, and Ser) or part (Trp) eventually form pyruvate, and Asn and Asp eventually form oxaloacetate, which are substrates of gluconeogenesis. ATP production varies from one amino acid to another (Table 11.1) with an average of about 22 ATP generated. The nitrogen (approximately 90%) in amino acids can be safely excreted from the body after it is catabolized and converted to urea.

氨基酸，蛋白质分解的产物，可以按照各自分解代谢途径分解产生能量。组成人体蛋白质的 21 种氨基酸首先可以通过脱氨基、转氨基、氧化脱氨基和非氧化脱氨基等方式来解离其氨基，然后它们进入糖类和脂类的有氧代谢途径，分解为 CO_2 并产生 ATP（图 11.2）。

所有的丙氨酸（半胱氨酸、甘氨酸、丝氨酸和部分色氨酸）最终可转换为丙酮酸，天冬酰胺和天冬氨酸转化为草酰乙酸，作为糖异生的底物。不同的氨基酸生成的 ATP 数量不同（表 11.1），平均约 22 个 ATP。氨基酸中的氮（约占 90%）在转变为尿素后可以安全地从体内排出。

11.2 Exercise and Protein Metabolism
运动与蛋白质代谢

11.2.1 Effects of Exercise on Protein Metabolism
运动对蛋白质代谢的影响

After an overnight fast, the normal average rate of muscle protein synthesis is 0.05% per hour, while the rate of muscle protein breakdown is 0.09% per hour. There is a negative protein balance (Figure 11.3). The effect of exercise on the synthesis and breakdown of protein in muscles depends on the type and intensity of exercise.

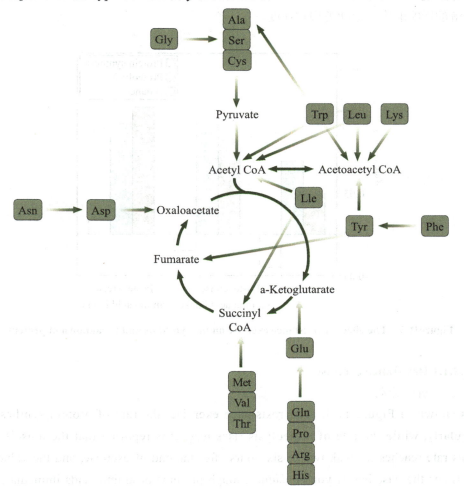

Figure 11.2　The catabolism of amino acid

Table 11.1　Energy yield of the complete oxidation of amino acids

Amino acid	ATP	Amino acid	ATP	Amino acid	ATP
Ala	12.5	Gly	12.5	Pro	25.0
Arg	25.0	His	22.5	Ser	12.5
Asn	12.5	Lle	29.0	Thr	19.0
Asp	12.5	Leu	31.0	Trp	45.0
Cys	12.5	Lys	22.5	Tyr	33.0
Gln	22.5	Met	19.0	Val	19.0
Glu	22.5	Phe	30.5	Average	22.0

正常情况下，经过一夜的禁食后，肌肉蛋白的平均合成速率为每小时 0.05%，而肌肉

蛋白的分解速率为每小时 0.09%，形成蛋白质的负平衡（图 11.3）。运动对肌肉蛋白质合成和分解的影响取决于运动类型和强度。

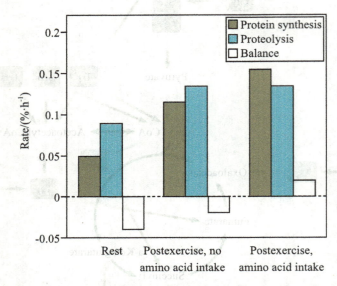

Figure11.3   The effect of resistance exercise on the synthesis and breakdown of protein

11.2.1.1 Resistance exercise
抗阻运动

As shown in Figure 11.3, after resistance exercise, the rate of protein synthesis rises spectacularly, while the rate of proteolysis rises less. It is reported that the muscle protein synthesis rate reaches its peak two to six hours after the end of exercise, and the value is two to four times the baseline. If you consume enough proteins or amino acids immediately after resistance exercise, muscle protein synthesis can remain above the baseline for up to two days after resistance exercise. Proteolysis is not affected significantly by dietary intake, which results in a shift of protein balance from negative to positive.

如图 11.3 所示，抗阻运动后，蛋白质合成率会显著上升，而蛋白质分解率上升幅度较小。据报道，运动结束后 2~6 h，肌肉蛋白合成率达到峰值，是基线的 2~4 倍。如果在抗阻运动后即刻摄入足够的蛋白质或氨基酸，骨骼肌的蛋白质合成速率可以在抗阻运动后的两天内保持在基线水平之上。蛋白质分解不受蛋白质摄入量的显著影响，这有利于加速蛋白质负平衡向正品平衡的转变。

In the case of same amount of exercise, the anabolic effect increases with the exercise intensity, and becomes stable at 60%–90% of one-repetition maximum (1RM). Nevertheless, if the total energy of low intensity resistance exercise is greater than that of high intensity resistance exercise, the rate of muscle protein synthesis can be also increased.

对比不同强度的抗阻运动，在保持总工作量不变的情况下，合成代谢效应随运动强度的增加而增加，直至 1 次重复最大重量（1RM）的 60%~90% 时趋于稳定。然而，如果一个人在低强度时所做的总功大于在高强度时所做的总功，那么肌肉蛋白的合成率也可以提高。

11.2.1.2 Endurance Exercise

耐力运动

According to reports, if we ingest adequate amount of proteins, the rate of muscle protein synthesis usually rises to no more than double the baseline immediately or within a few hours after an endurance exercise session, and remains above baseline for about one day. However, it is noteworthy that the rate of muscle proteolysis accelerates significantly faster than protein synthesis after endurance exercise, unless protein or amino acid supplements are consumed (Figure 11.4).

据报道，如果我们摄入足够的蛋白质，肌肉蛋白质的合成速度通常在耐力锻炼后不久或几小时内可达到基线水平的两倍，并在一天之内会保持在基线水平之上。需要注意的是，耐力训练后肌肉蛋白水解的速度往往比蛋白质合成的速度快得多，除非我们摄入蛋白质或氨基酸补充剂来加以调节（图 11.4）。

Protein status can be affected by carbohydrate adequacy but not by fat adequacy. In particular, if liver glycogen is depleted because of inadequate carbohydrate intake, the body will be deprived of its major source of blood glucose and subsequently resorts to proteins.

蛋白质的作用受到机体糖储备的影响，但不受脂肪含量的影响。特别是在糖摄入不足导致肝糖原耗竭时，机体失去了血糖的主要来源，从而转向蛋白质。

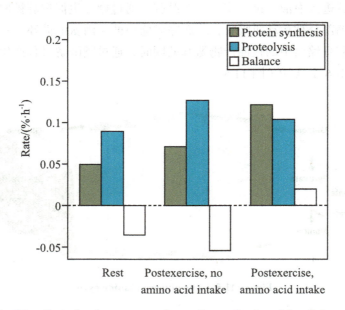

Figure11.4 The effect of endurance exercise on the synthesis and breakdown of protein

11.2.2 Effects of Exercise on Amino Acid Metabolism
运动对氨基酸代谢的影响

The total amino acid concentration in plasma is 3–4 mmol/L, which is not affected considerably by exercise lasting less than one hour. When exercise duration exceeds 2 hours, the plasma amino acid concentration drops as much as 30%. During exercise, the oxidation of leucine, isoleucine and valine (known collectively as branched-chain amino acids, BCAA) increases in muscle to provide energy for exercise. But the amino acid catabolism in muscle does not facilitate ATP resynthesis through carbohydrate or lipid catabolism.

血浆中氨基酸总浓度为 3~4 mmol/L，运动不足 1 h 对血浆氨基酸总浓度影响不大。当运动时间超过 2 h，血浆氨基酸浓度可下降 30%。在运动过程中，肌肉中的亮氨酸、异亮氨酸和缬氨酸（统称为支链氨基酸，BCAA）氧化分解增加以提供能量。但肌肉中的氨基酸分解代谢并不利于通过糖类或脂类的分解代谢促进 ATP 的再合成。

Amino acids from muscle can also be used as precursors for glucose synthesis in the liver. During exercise, the increase in skeletal muscle alanine production and the resulting increased liberation of alanine in the bloodstream result in a greater contribution to glucose synthesis through gluconeogenesis in the liver. Part of the glucose produced is taken up by the exercising muscles, thereby completing the glucose-alanine cycle. While relieving muscle amino groups, the glucose-alanine cycle can produce 2 ATPs through glycolysis and charge 6 ATP to the liver through gluconeogenesis in each turn of the cycle (Figure 11.5).

肌肉中的氨基酸也可以作为肝脏中葡萄糖合成的前体。运动期间，骨骼肌的丙氨酸生成量增加，并释放进入血液，进一步转运至肝脏，通过糖异生促进肝糖原的合成。肝糖原分解产生的葡萄糖部分被运动肌吸收，从而完成葡萄糖 – 丙氨酸循环。一次葡萄糖 – 丙氨酸循环可以在转移骨骼肌中的代谢产物氨基的同时，通过糖酵解过程产生 2 个 ATP，通过糖异生从肝脏获得 6 个 ATP（图 11.5）。

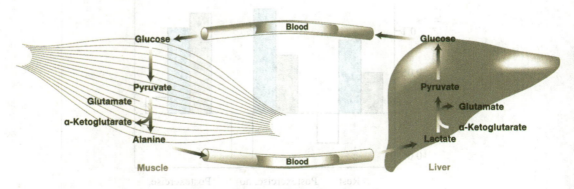

Figure 11.5 The glucose-alanine cycle

The rate of urea production appears to be related to exercise duration and intensity. It will not change during short-term vigorous exercise, but will increase during prolonged exercise. The plasma urea concentration also increases in exercise that lasts at least half an hour with the intensity at least 60% of $\dot{V}O_2max$.

尿素的生成速度与运动时间和运动强度有关。在短时间剧烈运动中，尿素不会发生变化，但在长时间运动中会上升。以 60% $\dot{V}O_2max$ 的运动强度持续运动至少半小时，血浆中的尿素浓度会随之增加。

11.2.3 Effects of Training on Muscle Remodeling
运动训练对肌肉重塑的影响

Muscle remodeling, the reorganization of muscle structure and function in response to training, plays an important role in maintaining both health and performance.

肌肉重塑是运动训练引起的骨骼肌结构和功能的重组，在维持机体健康和机能的过程中发挥重要的作用。

11.2.3.1 Resistance Training
抗阻训练

When accompanied by adequate protein intake, repeated sessions of resistance exercise will result in an accumulation of muscle protein, primarily myofibrillar proteins. This accumulation can cause the muscle hypertrophy (increased cross-sectional area of muscle fibers) include a few weeks after training started. After five to six months of resistance training, the muscle cross-section can increase by an average of 33%. Resistance training also promotes the maximum muscle strength, which has traditionally been attributed to muscle hypertrophy.

当伴有足够的蛋白质摄入时，反复的抗阻运动会引起肌肉（特别是肌纤维中的蛋白）累积。这种累积会在训练开始几周后引起肌肉肥大（肌肉纤维横截面积的增加）。经过 5~6 个月的抗阻训练，肌肉横截面平均增加 33%。抗阻训练还可以提高肌肉的最大力量，传统上认为这是肌肉肥大的原因。

There is a dose-effect relationship between the number of weekly sets of exercises and the degree of muscle hypertrophy. In order to maximize muscle hypertrophy, the major muscle groups should be trained at least two days per week. The strength gains are higher with five or more sets weekly than those lesser, although no additional strength gains seem to exist above nine sets. Compared to intensities of 60% or less, intensities above 60% of 1RM tend to produce greater muscle growth and strength gains. Nevertheless, training muscle groups once a week with an intensity between 20% and 60% of 1RM can still promote robust muscle hypertrophy, which may be much safer for novices. The time taken to complete a repetition does not seem to influence hypertrophy. Interruption or cessation of training, will lead to a gradual loss of muscle mass gains.

每周锻炼的次数与肌肉肥大程度呈现剂量效应关系。为了达到最大限度的肌肉肥大，每周至少应该有 2 天进行主要肌群的抗阻训练。每周 5 次或 5 次以上的抗阻训练可以获得更大的肌肉力量，但每周9次以上的训练不会带来更多的力量增长。大于60% 1RM 的运动强度比小于或等于60% 1RM 的强度更有利于促进肌肉的生长和肌肉力量的增加。然而，每周对一个肌群进行一次 20%~60% 1RM 强度的训练，仍然可以促进正常的肌肉肥大，这对于刚开始抗阻训练的个体来说可能更安全。完成一组重复训练所花的时间似乎对肌肉肥大的效果没有影响。间断训练或停止训练会导致增加的肌肉逐渐减少。

11.2.3.2 Endurance Training
耐力训练

Endurance training is usually not accompanied by muscle hypertrophy. But some high intensity endurance training may cause certain increase in myofibrillar proteins and a small degree of hypertrophy. It is reported that the increase in muscle mitochondrial proteins with endurance training leads to an increase in the volume of the mitochondrial reticulum. Mitochondrial content accounts for about 4% (ranging from 2% to 6%) in untrained human skeletal muscle can be increased by about 50% (to 6% on average, and range from 4% to 8%) after a few (for example, six) weeks of endurance training. The exercise-induced increase in mitochondrial content allows muscles to regenerate a larger portion of the ATP needed for exercise through the aerobic breakdown of carbohydrates, lipids, and proteins. This process is more economical than the anaerobic breakdown of carbohydrates and increases resistance to fatigue.

耐力训练通常不会伴随肌肉肥大。但是在高强度训练时，耐力训练会引起部分肌原纤维蛋白含量增加和小幅度的肥大。耐力训练可增加肌肉线粒体蛋白质含量，进而引起线粒体网体积的增加。在未经训练个体的骨骼肌中，线粒体数量约为4%（从2%~6% 不等），经过几周（比如6周）的耐力训练后，线粒体含量可增加近50%（平均含量为6%，从4%~8% 不等）。运动引起的线粒体含量增加，使肌肉可以通过糖类、脂类和蛋白质的有氧分解获得运动所需的更多的ATP。这个过程比糖类的无氧分解更经济，增强了机体的抗疲劳能力。

11.2.4 Contribution of Proteins to the Energy Expenditure of Exercise
运动中的蛋白质供能

The role of protein in ATP resynthesis during short-term exercise of any intensity is negligible, and the energy contribution of protein to prolonged (even ultra-prolonged) exercise is about 3% to 6% of total energy expenditure. Thus, protein contributes little to energy expenditure during exercise.

在任何强度的短时间运动中，蛋白质在 ATP 再合成中的作用都是微不足道的。而且在长时间（甚至是超长时间）运动中，蛋白质的供能作用约占总能量消耗的3%~6%。因此，蛋白质对运动中的能量贡献很小。

11.3 Exercise and Protein Supplementation
运动与蛋白质补充

Generally, athletes and people who exercise regularly have higher protein requirements than individuals who do not do exercise. Therefore, although the daily recommended intake for the general adult population is 0.8 g/kg body mass, the American College of Sports Medicine, Academy of Nutrition and Dietetics, and the Dietitians of Canada—issued a joint position statement recommending 1.2–1.4 g/kg for persons who engaged in endurance training and 1.2–1.7 g/kg for persons who performed resistance training. It is reported that protein supplementation during prolonged (at least six–week) resistance exercise improved muscle hypertrophy and maximum strength (1RM).

一般来说，运动员和经常锻炼的人比不锻炼的人对蛋白质的需求更高。因此，尽管一般成年人的蛋白质每日推荐摄入量为 0.8 g/kg 体重，美国运动医学学会、美国营养和食品学会和加拿大的营养学家联合声明，建议从事耐力训练的人每天每千克体重应摄入蛋白质 1.2~1.4 g；进行抗阻训练的人每天每千克体重应摄入蛋白质 1.2~1.7 g。据报导，在长时间（至少 6 周）的抗阻运动中，补充蛋白质可以改善肌肉肥大和增加最大力量（1RM）。

Protein supplementation can be achieved in a variety of ways. The keys include that protein can be easily digestible, the amino acids can be delivered efficiently to muscles, and a high ratio of essential aminoacids to non-essential amino acids. Among the essential amino acids, leucine possesses the highest anabolic potential. The highest known leucine content is found in whey protein. Among plant-derived foods, maize protein is believed to contain the highest proportion of leucine.

蛋白质的补充可以通过多种方式实现。其中，蛋白质的易消化吸收性非常重要，骨骼肌氨基酸输送效率，以及必需氨基酸与非必需氨基酸的高比值也是关键。在必需氨基酸中，亮氨酸具有最高的合成代谢潜力。乳清蛋白中的亮氨酸含量最高。在植物性食物中，玉米蛋白中的亮氨酸含量最多。

Chapter 12　Metabolic Regulation in Exercise

第十二章　运动中的代谢调节

12.1 Integration of Exercise Metabolism
运动代谢的整合

In the previous chapters, we have known that the metabolism of carbohydrates, lipids or proteins is always interacted with each other (Figure 12.1). The interaction of metabolic pathways during exercise is often taught as an energy continuum.

Due to the limited quantity of most sources, energy sources during maximum exercise (Figure 12.2 A) and prolonged exercise (Figure 12.2 B) will not remain stable even if the intensity is stable. There is hardly to say any kind of exercise that does not require a considerable contribution of energy from at least two categories. Exercise intensity and duration affect the proportion of energy sources in opposite ways (Figure 12.3).

在前几章中，我们已经知道糖类、脂类或蛋白质的代谢是相互交织的（图 12.1）。运动过程中代谢途径的相互作用通常被视为连续能区。

由于大多数供能物质的数量有限，即使强度稳定，在极量运动（图 12.2 A）和长时间运动（图 12.2 B）时的能量来源也不稳定。任何一种都需要至少两种能量来源。而运动强度和持续时间对供能物质的供能比例的影响是相反的（图 12.3）。

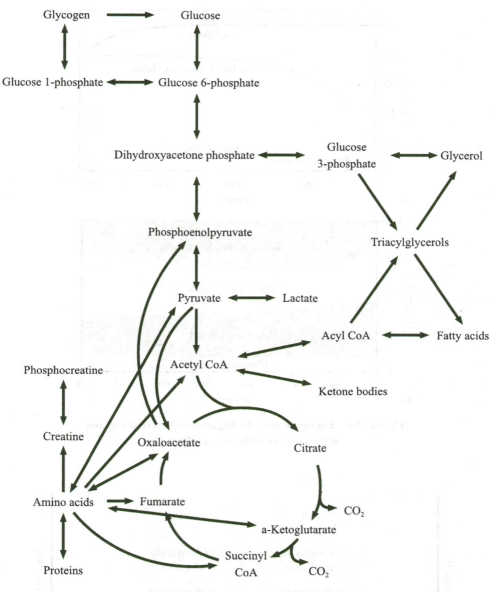

Figure 12.1 Interconnections of carbohydrates, lipids or proteins metabolism

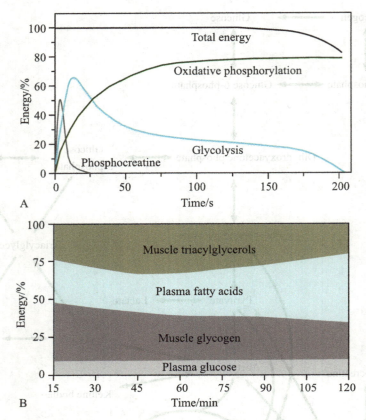

Figure 12.2   Energy sources during maximal exercise (A) and 65% VO₂max endurance cycling (B)

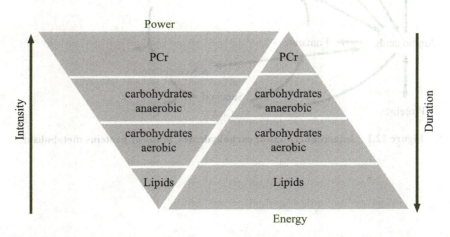

Figure 12.3   Choice of energy sources depending on the exercise intensity and duration

12.2 Interconversion of Lipids and Carbohydrates
糖类与脂类的相互转化

As we know, most of ATP consumed during exercise comes from the metabolism of carbohydrates and lipids. Carbohydrates possess the advantage of faster ATP resynthesis, while lipids have the advantage of a larger energy store. Thus, athletes intend to have body fat as same as the carbohydrate stores. However, fatty acids are unable to produce glucose, and there is too little glycerol that can be converted into glucose in the liver and kidneys, which has little contribution to the provision of carbohydrates. Therefore, lipids cannot adequately replenish carbohydrates, and proper nutrition must be used to ensure adequate carbohydrates in the body. On the other hand, the abundance of carbohydrate facilitates the complete oxidation of fatty acids and reduces the formation of ketone bodies; the shortage of carbohydrates stimulates gluconeogenesis of pyruvate or oxaloacetate and increases the formation of ketone bodies (Figure 12.4).

正如我们所知道的，运动所需要的大部分 ATP 是由糖类和脂类的代谢提供的，糖类具有再合成 ATP 速度快的优点，而脂类则具有储存能量多的优点。因此，运动员希望体内储存的糖类能够与脂肪一样多。但是脂肪酸不能产生葡萄糖，可以在肝脏和肾脏中转化为葡萄糖的甘油又太少，不能对糖类的供应产生明显的影响。因此，脂类完全不能替代糖类，必须通过适当的营养措施来保证体内的糖类充足。另一方面，糖储备充足有利于脂肪酸的完全氧化，减少酮体的生成；缺少糖可激活丙酮酸或草酰乙酸的糖异生作用，使酮体生成增加（图 12.4）。

The amount of carbohydrates and lipids that fuel prolonged exercise depends on exercise intensity (Figure 12.5). During rest and light exercise, most of the energy needed by the whole body comes from breakdown of lipids. When the exercise intensity is around 50% of $\dot{V}O_2max$, the energy coming from the carbohydrate breakdown will catch up with the energy coming from the lipid breakdown. At higher exercise intensity, carbohydrate breakdown rises sharply, while lipid breakdown drops.

为长期运动提供能量的糖类和脂类的数量取决于运动强度（图 12.5）。在休息和低强度运动时，整个身体消耗的大部分能量来自脂质分解。在运动强度为 50% $\dot{V}O_2max$ 左右时，糖类分解产生的能量会赶上脂质分解产生的能量。在高强度运动时，糖类分解急剧增加，而脂质分解减少。

The intensity at which fat is oxidized at the maximum rate (maximum fat oxidation, MFO) is usually symbolized as Fat_{max}. Fat_{max} ranges from 40% to 70% of $\dot{V}O_2max$, and MFO ranges from 0.4 to 0.7 g/min for most healthy and lean individuals. The higher Fat_{max} and MFO mean better aerobic endurance performance and health condition. In terms of performance, higher Fat_{max} means that endurance athletes can burn a lot of fat during high-intensity exercise exercise, thereby sparing carbohydrates. In terms of health, high MFO is considered to prevent metabolic

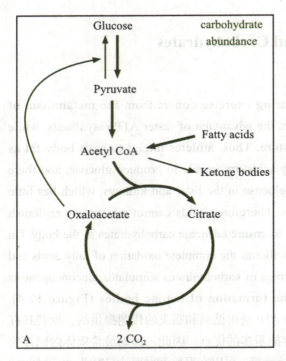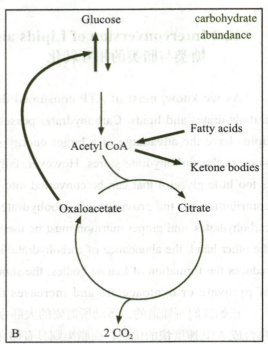

Figure 12.4 Interconversion of lipids and carbohydrates

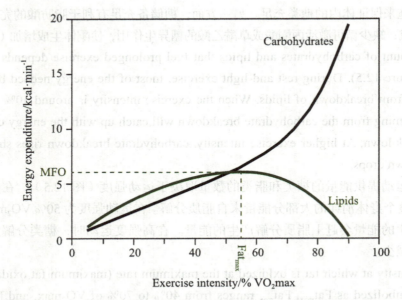

Figure 12.5 The energy supply relationship of carbohydrates and lipids at different exercise intensities

perturbations.

脂肪以最大速率氧化（最大脂肪氧化率，MFO）时所对应的运动强度，通常用 Fat_{max} 表示。对于大多数健康和苗条的人来说，Fat_{max} 一般为 40%~70% $\dot{V}O_2max$，最大脂肪氧化速率为 0.4~0.7 g/min；最大脂肪氧化速率和 Fat_{max} 越高，说明有氧耐力表现和健康水平越好。就表现而言，最大脂肪氧化速率对应的运动强度越高，意味着耐力运动员可以在高运动强度下燃烧大量脂肪，从而节省了糖。在健康方面，较高的最大脂肪氧化速率有助于防止代谢紊乱。

12.3 Adaptation of Training
训练适应

The adaptations of different training programs are diverse (Table 12.1). There are individual differences in response to a given training program or training dose. Therefore, the effects of different training programs on different people need to elicit a significant response to promote performance and health. On the other hand, adaptations to training are not permanent. Maintaining adaptations requires regular application of a substantial training stimulus.

机体对不同训练方案产生的适应性不同（表 12.1）。对特定训练计划或训练剂量的反应存在个体差异。因此，以提高身体机能和健康水平为目的的运动训练计划，需要针对个体差异分别制订。另一方面，机体对训练的适应性变化并不是永久的。要保持适应性变化，需要进行有规律的实质性训练刺激。

Table 12.1   Adaptations of exercise metabolism to different types of training

Training Type	Adaptation
Endurance Training	The muscle mitochondrial content increases
	Glucose uptake decreases
	The rate of muscle glycogenolysis decreases
	Fatty acid uptake increases
	$\dot{V}O_2max$ increase
Resistance Training	Muscle hypertrophy
	Increase in maximal strength
Sprint Training	Increase in muscle adenylate kinase and creatine kinase
	Increase in muscle phosphorylase, phosphofructokinase, and lactate dehydrogenase
	Increase in muscle mitochondrial enzymes
Interval Training	$\dot{V}O_2max$ increase
	Muscle mitochondrial content and mitochondrial enzymes increase
	Resting muscle glycogen increase
	Muscle glycogenolysis and lactate production decrease during exercise at a given absolute intensity

12.3.1 Adaptation of Endurance Training

耐力训练的适应

Long-term endurance exercise increases the contribution of plasma FFA to energy supply and reduces the reliance of muscle on both muscle glycogen and intramuscular triglyceride (Figure 12.6). The most spectacular adaptation of endurance training is a shift of mainly energy supplement from carbohydrate to lipid oxidation at a given absolute exercise intensity (Figure 12.7), so as to prolong exercise and spare carbohydrates. Thus, athletes can exercise at a higher intensity while spending the same amount of carbohydrates, which is followed by an increase in $\dot{V}O_2$max and improvement in aerobic endurance performance and cardiorespiratory fitness (CRF).

长期的耐力运动可以增加血浆游离脂肪酸的供能比例，降低对肌糖原和肌内脂肪的依赖（图12.6）。耐力训练引起的最显著的适应性变化是在特定的绝对强度下运动时，供能物质从糖类氧化向脂类氧化的转变（图12.7），从而在延长运动时间的同时节省了糖。因此，运动员可以在消耗相同糖的情况下完成更高强度的运动，从而提高机体的最大摄氧量，提高有氧耐力表现和心肺适能（CRF）。

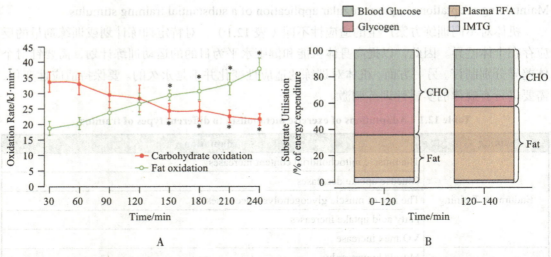

Figure 12.6 **Whole body CHO and lipid oxidation rates (A) and relative contribution of muscle and blood-borne substrates to energy production (B) during prolonged exercise at 57% $\dot{V}O_2$max IMTGs: intra-muscular triglycerides**

The change in the proportion of energy sources during exercise caused by endurance training derives from skeletal muscle adaptations. For example, endurance training increases the muscle FFA uptake and intra-muscular triglycerides utilization, but it does not increase adipose tissue lipolysis. On the other hand, the increase of the rest muscle glycogen content from 20% to 60% induced by endurance training may be due to the muscle insulin sensitivity improvement caused by exercise, although the liver glycogen content does not change. The increase in $\dot{V}O_2$max primarily comes from circulatory adaptations.

　　耐力训练引起的运动中供能物质供能比例的变化源于骨骼肌的适应（耐力训练增加了肌肉游离脂肪酸的摄取和肌内脂肪的利用，但不增加脂肪组织的脂肪分解）。另一方面，耐力训练可使安静时的肌糖原含量上升 20%~66%，这可能是因为锻炼增强了肌肉对胰岛素作用的敏感性，但肝糖原含量似乎没有变化。最大摄氧量的增加主要是循环适应的结果。

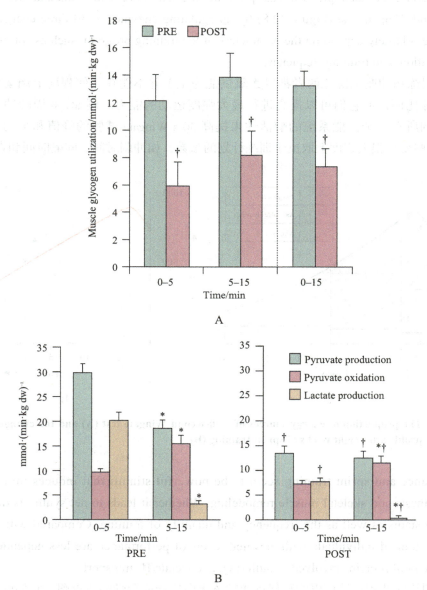

Figure12.7　Muscle glycogen utilization (A) and the fate of pyruvate and lactate (B) during 15 minutes of exercise at 80% $\dot{V}O_2$max undertaken before and after seven weeks of endurance training

12.3.2 Adaptation of Resistance and Sprint Training
抗阻训练和冲刺训练的适应

Resistance or strength training and sprint training (both heavily rely on anaerobic energy metabolism) do not modulate the proportion of energy sources during exercise to any considerable extent, but they can result in an increase in the ability to perform the maximum intensity exercise. For example, 8 weeks sprint training can improve the peak and mean power of the 30-second Wingate test (Figure 12.8) by upregulating enzymes of all three energy systems. These changes largely depend on the parameters of the training program, such as sprint duration, interval duration, and training frequency.

抗阻训练和冲刺训练（两者都以无氧供能为主）并不能在任何程度上调运动过程中的能量来源比例，但它们可以提高进行最大强度运动的能力。例如，8 周的冲刺训练可以通过上调所有三个供能系统的酶活性来提高 30 s Wingate 试验的峰值和平均功率（图 12.8）。这些变化很大程度上取决于训练计划的参数，如冲刺时间、间隔时间和训练频率。

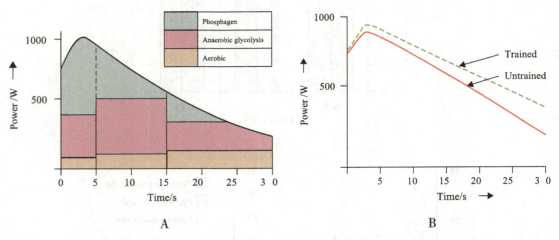

Figure 12.8　The proportion of energy sources of a 30-second Wingate test (A) and the changes of power profile after eight weeks of sprint training (B)

Resistance and sprint training seem to be powerful stimuli that induces mitochondrial protein synthesis and skeletal muscle remodeling. Whether it leads to net synthesis depends on the training status as well as the frequency and quantity of training. Compared with untrained individuals, trained individuals with elevated levels of performance are less dependent on the muscle content of proteins involved in buffering, and lactate/H^+ transport.

抗阻训练和冲刺训练可以明显促进线粒体蛋白质合成和骨骼肌重塑，它们的作用效果取决于训练状态、训练的频率和数量。与未受过训练的个体相比，那些受过训练且运动表现更佳的个体，对于肌肉中参与缓冲作用和乳酸 /H^+ 转运的蛋白质依赖性更小。

12.3.3 Adaptation of Interval Training
间歇训练的适应

There are two types of interval training, high-intensity interval training (HIIT) and sprint interval training (SIT). HIIT involves the submaximal intensity that elicits at least 80% of HRmax. Frequently used and effective HIIT protocol includes four bouts of 4 min exercise at 85% to 95% of HRmax, separated by 3 to 4 min of passive recovery. SIT involves maximal efforts or an exercise intensity corresponding to at least 100% of the power corresponding to $\dot{V}O_2$max. Frequently used and effective SIT protocol involves four to six all-out bouts of 30 s, separated by 4 min of active or passive recovery. Depending on the specific circumstances of the training protocol, these interventions can be further classified as speed/sprint, speed endurance, or high-intensity aerobic interval training. In all cases, the recommended training frequency is three times per week. It is reported that athletes repeatedly performed 15 × 40 m maximal sprints and the recovery between sprints was 30, 60 or 120 s, respectively. The decline in sprint performance is greatest with 30 s of recovery, and post-exercise blood lactate and plasma hypoxanthine are also greatest in this condition. Therefore, subtle differences in the intensity and duration of both the interval and recovery periods can affect the metabolic responses to the HIIT protocol. But, it is consensus that higher intensity activities will lead to greater depletion, and greater durations of recovery will lead to greater resynthesis. If the purpose of training is to develop the speed, then the intensity of the sprints should be maximized with a duration of less than 10 s, in order to focus on using PCr hydrolysis and glycolysis as the main contributors to ATP turnover. Similarly, the recovery between sprints should be at least 60 s, to maximize PCr resynthesis and restore muscle pH. If the purpose of training is to develop the speed endurance (continuous production of high speed for a sustained period), the duration of the interval should be increased to approximately 30 to 90 s (with approximately an equal recovery period) in order to tax fully exercise glycolytic and oxidative systems. If the purpose of training is to maximize the development of the aerobic system (both oxygen uptake and oxidative capacity of skeletal muscle), the intensity and duration of the interval should be close to $\dot{V}O_2$max for 2 to 4 min, with 2 to 3 min of active recovery.

间歇训练分为两类：高强度间歇训练（HIIT）和冲刺间歇训练（SIT）。高强度间歇训练采用至少 80% 最大心率的次最大强度。常用的且有效的高强度间歇训练方案是在 85%~95% 最大心率的强度下进行 4 组、每组 4 min 的间歇运动，组间间隔 3~4 min 的被动恢复；冲刺间歇训练采用至少 100% $\dot{V}O_2$max 的强度进行最大负荷运动。常用且有效的冲刺间歇训练方案包括 4~6 组的 30 s 的全力运动，组间间隔 4 min 的主动或被动恢复。根据训练方案的具体情况，这些干预措施可以进一步分为速度 / 冲刺、速度耐力或高强度有氧间歇训练。在所有情况下，推荐的训练频率是每周 3 次。据报道，运动员反复进行 15 次 40 m 的最大冲刺，每次冲刺之间的间歇时间分别为 30 s、60 s、120 s。在间歇 30 s 时短跑成绩下降最大，运动后的血乳酸和血浆次黄嘌呤含量最高。因此，高强度间歇训练方案在干预期和恢复期的运动强度和持续时间的细微差异就可以引起代谢的变化。一般认为，运动强度越大能量消耗越多，恢复时间越长，再合成越多。如果训练的目的是发展速度，那么冲刺的强度应该是最大的，持续时间应该小于 10 s，以便集中利用 PCr 水解和糖酵解作为 ATP 再合成的主要途径。同样地，冲刺之间的恢复时间至少应为 60 s，以最大限度地实现 PCr 的重新合成，恢复肌肉的 pH 值。如果训练目标是发展速度耐力（长时间维持较高的速度），那么运动的持续时间应该延长到 30~90 s（约等于间歇时间），以最大限度地动员糖酵解和氧化系统。如果训练的目的是最大限度地发展有氧系统（骨骼肌的氧吸收和氧化能力），那么就应该选择 2~4 min 的接近最大摄氧量强度的运动，并在 2~3 min 的间歇进行积极恢复。

HIIT consists of both high-intensity (near maximal or ultra-maximal activity) as well as low to moderate intensity activities. ATP production is fuelled by both anaerobic and aerobic systems, and in the latter case, carbohydrate is the predominant substrate. Lipid oxidation is also important, especially in the recovery period between high-intensity exercise and when the exercise period becomes prolonged. There is a common misconception that HIE is mainly fueled by the anaerobic system, specifically anaerobic glycolysis. In fact, both the aerobic and anaerobic systems are activated from the onset of exercise, and the contribution of the aerobic system becomes more important as the duration of the exercise increases (Figure 12.9). Therefore, athletes involved in high-intensity interval sports should have a well-developed aerobic system and high maximum oxygen uptake to ensure high rates of oxygen delivery and utilization of the exercising muscles.

高强度间歇训练包括高强度（接近最大或超最大强度活动）和低至中等强度的活动，ATP 的再合成需要无氧和有氧供能系统同时参与。在有氧供能系统中，糖类是主要的底物。脂质氧化也很重要，特别是在高强度运动之间的恢复期以及运动时间延长的时候。有一个普遍的误解，认为高强度间歇训练主要是由无氧供能系统，特别是无氧糖酵解供能的。事实上，有氧和无氧系统从运动一开始就都被激活，随着运动持续时间的增加，有氧供能系统的作用变得更加重要（图 12.9）。因此，参与高强度间歇运动的运动员应该有良好的有氧供能能力和较高的最大摄氧量，以确保运动肌具有较高的氧转运率和利用率。

High intensity interval training elicits some favorable adaptations associated with moderate-intensity continuous training (MICT). These adaptations include an increase in muscle mitochondrial content, $\dot{V}O_2$max, the ratio of lipids to oxidized carbohydrates, and a decrease in muscle glycogenolysis and lactate production during exercise at a fixed absolute moderate intensity. The adaptations also include the increase in resting muscle glycogen content and an improvement in aerobic endurance performance. Athletes can achieve these adaptations by spending less total time (including intervals) and less net exercise time compared with MICT. Thus, high intensity interval training is considered a time-efficient alternative to MICT for both athletes and the general population, although it has higher physical demands than MICT because it involves high exercise intensity.

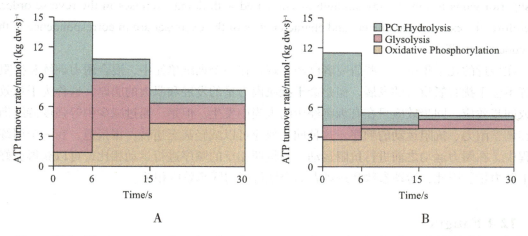

Figure 12.9 The energy supply ratio of each energy supply system during bout 1 (A) and bout 3 (B)

高强度间歇训练可以引起一些与中等强度持续训练（MICT）相关的良性适应。这些适应包括在一个固定的绝对中等强度的运动中，肌肉线粒体含量增加，最大摄氧量增加，脂肪和糖类的氧化比例增加，肌肉糖原分解和乳酸产生减少；安静时，肌肉糖原含量增加和有氧耐力表现改善等。与中等强度持续训练相比，一个人可以用更少的总时间（包括间隔时间）和更少的运动时间来实现这些适应性变化。因此，对于运动员和普通人群来说，高强度间歇训练被认为是替代中等强度持续训练的一种时间效率高的方法。但由于它采用的是高强度运动，需要运动者具有较强的运动能力。

12.3.4 Adaptation of Concurrent Training
组合训练的适应

Athletes and exercisers often engage in more than one type of training to get even more favorable adaptations. In a periodic training program, endurance and resistance exercise are performed separately, or combined in a session and performed alternately, which is described as concurrent training.

为了获得更好的适应能力，运动员和锻炼者经常进行不止一种训练。在一个阶段性的训练计划中，耐力训练和抗阻训练分别在各自独立的单元中进行，或者在一个单元中交替进行，这称为组合训练。

In recent decades, several researchers have found that mixed endurance and resistance exercises in a training session do not interfere with the development of aerobic endurance, but the strength development and muscle hypertrophy, which is termed the interference effect, or concurrent effect. A concurrent effect dose not occur in untrained person but in trained ones. However, the concurrent effect can be mitigated or even reversed by decreasing the work of MICT and regulating the execution sequence of endurance and resistance exercises. It is reported that performing resistance exercise before endurance exercise in a training session can result in superior gains in lower-body strength as compared with doing exercises in the reverse order. Therefore, the exercise parameters and characteristics of the exerciser are in correspondence with the concurrent effect.

在最近的几十年里，一些研究者已经发现，在一个训练单元中，混合耐力训练和抗阻训练不会干扰有氧耐力的发展，但是会干扰肌肉力量的发展和肌肉的肥厚，这称为干扰效应或同步效应。同步效应只在有训练经历的人当中发生。但是，通过减少中等强度持续训练和调整耐力、抗阻运动的顺序，这种同步效应可以减轻甚至逆转。据报道，在一个训练过程中，在耐力运动之前进行抗阻运动，与按照相反的顺序进行运动相比，可以获得更好的下肢力量。因此，运动参数和运动者的个性特征与同步效应相关。

12.4 Fatigue
疲劳

12.4.1 Definition and Classification of Fatigue
疲劳的定义及分类

Fatigue is traditionally defined as the failure to maintain the required or expected exercise status, and it is divided into central fatigue (emanating from the central nervous system) and peripheral fatigue (resulting from inability of the motor unit to perform). Because the traditional definition ignores the sensation of fatigue in the exerciser, and it is difficult to distinguish the decline in muscle force (recognized as peripheral fatigue) from the sensation related to fatigue (recognized as central fatigue), especially during prolonged exercise. Therefore, the fatigue is redefined as a disabling symptom in which physical and cognitive functions are limited by interactions between performance fatigability and perceived fatigability, and it is divided into performance fatigue and perceived fatigue. Performance fatigue depends on the contractile capability of active muscles and the ability of the nervous system to provide adequate activation signals; otherwise perceived fatigue depends on the initial value and the rate of change in sensations. These sensations regulate the integrity of the exercisers on the basis of maintaining their homeostasis and psychological state.

传统上，疲劳被定义为无法维持所需或预期的机能，分为中枢疲劳（由中枢神经系统引起的）和外周疲劳（由运动单元能力下降导致的）。因为传统的定义忽略了锻炼者的疲劳感，而且很难将肌肉力量的下降（被认为是外周疲劳）与疲劳相关的感觉（被认为是中枢疲劳）区分开来，尤其是在长时间的运动中。因此，疲劳被重新定义为一种身体和认知功能受到行为疲劳和感知疲劳相互作用而下降的现象，并被分为行为疲劳和感知疲劳。行为疲劳取决于运动肌的收缩能力和神经系统提供充分激活信号的能力；而感知疲劳取决于运动者保持体内平衡和心理状态的初始值和维持整体状态的变化幅度。

Muscle fatigue can be defined as an exercise induced reduction in the ability of muscles to produce force or power, regardless of whether the task can be sustained. This can be demonstrated by examining the power output curve of an individual through the 30-second Wingate test.

肌肉疲劳可以被定义为一种运动导致的肌肉做功能力下降，而与任务能否持续无关。可以通过 30 s Wingate 试验的功率输出结果来进行监测。

12.4.2 Mechanism of Exercise Fatigue
运动疲劳的机理

Although exercise fatigue has been extensively studied for more than a century, its cause remains largely unclear. In general, the onset of fatigue will vary depending on many factors, including fitness level and training status, exercise intensity, and environmental conditions (e.g., heat, humidity, and altitude). Moreover, the cause of fatigue in one type of exercise may be quite different from that in another. Table 12.2 summarizes the most likely causes of fatigue during exercise.

尽管运动疲劳已被广泛研究了一个多世纪，它的发生原因仍然在很大程度上不明确。总的来说，疲劳的发生取决于许多因素，包括体能水平和训练状态、运动强度和环境条件（如热、湿度和海拔）。此外，一项运动中的疲劳发生原因可能与另一项运动中疲劳发生的原因有很大的不同。表 12.2 总结了最可能导致运动疲劳的原因。

Table 12.2　Probable causes of fatigue during exercise depending on dominant energy system

Energy System	Causes of Fatigue
ATP–phosphocreatine system	Decreased motor unit firing rate Phosphocreatine depletion
Lactate system	Decreased motor unit firing rate Decreased muscle excitation Pi and H^+ accumulation
Oxygen system	Hypoglycemia Dehydration Hyperthermia Decreased muscle excitation Glycogen depletion Pi and H^+ accumulation RONS accumulation

As shown in Figure 12.10, at the fatigue point of high-intensity exercise (HIE), the concentration of cytoplasmic ATP does not drop below 60% of the resting level. But the concentrations of muscle PCr decrease significantly from 80 to 15 mmol/kg, and Pi and Lactic acid increase significantly in response to a single strenuous bout of HIE. The accumulation of Pi and lactic acid in muscles is considered to be the major cause of fatigue. Reduced carbohydrate availability (decreased ATP regeneration) may be the predominant underlying mechanism of fatigue induced by prolonged endurance exercise. The reduction of carbohydrates will not only reduce the rate of ATP regeneration, but the carbohydrates depletion will also lead to metabolic disturbances in the peripheral processes involved in muscle contraction.

　　如图 12.10 所示，在高强度运动中发生疲劳时，细胞质 ATP 浓度不会降低到安静水平的 60% 以下，但肌肉中磷酸肌酸的浓度会显著下降，从 80 mmol/kg 降低到 15 mmol/kg；磷酸和乳酸浓度会在一组高强度运动中显著增加。肌肉中磷酸和乳酸的积累被认为是疲劳的主要原因。糖利用率降低（降低了 ATP 的再合成率）可能是由长时间的耐力运动引起的疲劳的主要潜在机制。糖类的减少不仅降低了 ATP 再合成的速度，糖类的消耗还会导致与肌肉收缩相关的外周代谢过程的紊乱。

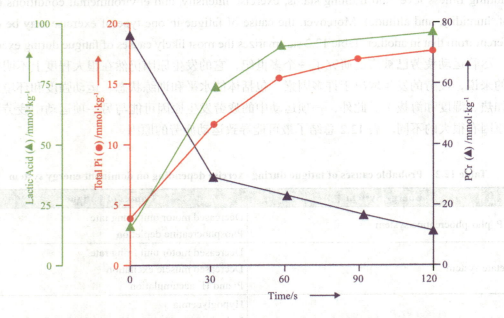

Figure 12.10　Changes in PCr, Pi and lactic acid due to a series of maximal muscle contractions

12.4.3 Recovery of Fatigue
疲劳恢复

When the training session or competition is over, it is expected that the body will return to its pre-exercise energy state as soon as possible in anticipation of new exercise tasks. The time needed to restore the energy state is generally longer than the duration of the exercise, because the replenishment of the energy source is slower than the consumption.

Due to metabolic factors, the nutritional status of participants plays a significant role in the ability to perform a prolonged exercise. Therefore, dietary conditioning and nutritional supplementation before, during and after exercise can accelerate the recovery of the body's energy state after exercise. The integration of training and nutritional strategies will not only accelerate recovery, but also improve performance.

当训练或比赛结束后，机体应尽快恢复到训练前的能量状态，为新的训练任务做好准备。机体恢复能量状态所需的时间通常比运动的时间要长，因为能量的补充比消耗要慢。

运动者的营养状况是影响机体代谢水平的重要因素，对运动能力起着重要的作用。因此，通过运动前、中、后的饮食调控和营养补充可以加速运动后机体能量状态的恢复。综合训练和营养策略不仅能加速恢复，而且有利于提高运动表现。

◯ Summary

ATP is the representative of the direct energy source. The ATP-ADP cycle is the main route of energy exchange in biological systems, which is maintained by ATP-phosphagen system, anaerobic glycolysis (lactate system) and aerobic system (oxygen system) during exercise to resynthesize ATP.

Carbohydrates, lipids, and proteins are fuels that supply (or replenish) direct energy source. Glycogenolysis and glycolysis are the main processes of carbohydrate breakdown. A lack of carbohydrates promotes the oxidation of triglycerides. The effects of exercise on metabolism of carbohydrates, lipids, and proteins are interrelated.

The energy provision for exercise is the smooth blending and overlapped of all three energy systems. The selection of energy source during exercise, replenishment of energy source after exercise, and the causes of fatigue are primarily determined by exercise parameters (such as exercises type, intensity, duration, and frequency), the characteristics of the exerciser (such as gender, age, nutritional state, training status, and the genome) and environmental factors (such as ambient temperature and hypoxia).

◯ 本篇小结

ATP 是直接能源的代表。ATP–ADP 循环是生物系统中能量交换的主要途径，在运动过程中由 ATP–磷酸肌酸系统、无氧糖酵解系统（乳酸系统）和有氧氧化系统再合成 ATP，以维持 ATP–ADP 循环。

糖类、脂类和蛋白质是直接能量来源的燃料。糖原分解和糖酵解是糖类分解的主要过程。糖类的缺乏会促进脂肪的氧化分解。运动对糖类、脂类和蛋白质代谢的影响是相互联系的。

运动训练的能量供应是由三个供能系统共同参与、交互作用的。运动中供能物质的选择、运动后供能物质的补充以及运动疲劳的发生，与运动参数（如运动类型、运动强度、持续时间和运动频率）、个体特征（如性别、年龄、营养状态、训练状态和基因）及环境因素（如环境温度、缺氧）等有关。

Part III　Exercise and Health
第三篇　运动与健康

○ **Learning Objectives**

· Outline the relationship between exercise and aging.
· Outline the relationship between exercise and body weight management.
· Outline the relationship between exercise and chronic metabolic diseases such as obesity, cardiovascular disease and diabetes and osteoporosis.

○ **学习目标**

·掌握运动与衰老的关系。
·掌握运动与体重管理的关系。
·掌握运动与肥胖、心血管疾病、糖尿病和骨质疏松症等慢性代谢疾病的关系。

The World Health Organization (WHO) defines health as not only the absence of disease or infirmity, but also the state of complete physical, mental, and social well-being. Ample and convincing epidemiological evidence indicates that physical inactivity increases morbidity and mortality of chronic diseases. WHO estimates that about 3.2 million people worldwide die each year due to lack of physical activity.

Regular exercise has been increasingly accepted and recognized as a powerful intervention that can reduce the morbidity and mortality of chronic diseases. Therefore, the American College of Sports Medicine (ACSM) and some international organizations recommended that people should do 150 min of moderate-intensity exercise, or 75 min of vigorous exercise, or a combination of both every week. Individuals who even do physical activity less than the minimum recommended amount have a 20% lower risk of death compared with individuals who do not. There is a dose-response relationship between physical activity and numerous health indicators, such as high-density lipoprotein, cholesterol and cardiorespiratory fitness. Individuals who meet or exceed the recommended amount of physical activity will get more health benefit.

世界卫生组织（WHO）对健康的定义不仅是没有疾病或体质不虚弱，而且是指人的身体、精神、社会功能各方面都处于良好的状态。大量令人信服的流行病学证据表明，缺乏身体活动会增加慢性疾病的发生率和死亡率。世界卫生组织估计，全世界每年约有 320 万人死于身体活动不足。

规律运动作为降低慢性疾病发生率及死亡率的一种强有力的干预手段，被广泛地接受和认可。美国运动医学学会（ACSM）和一些国际机构建议人们每周应该进行 150 min 的中等强度运动，或 75 min 的高强度运动，或两者结合。即使运动时间低于推荐的最低限度的运动人群，其死亡率也比完全不运动的人低 20％。身体活动与许多健康指标之间存在剂量效应关系，如高密度脂蛋白、胆固醇和心肺耐力。达到或超过身体活动推荐量最低值的个体可以获得更高的健康收益。

Chapter 13　Exercise and Aging

第十三章　运动与衰老

Aging is a natural and inevitable process for humans. Aging is not a disease, but it constitutes a risk factor for many diseases, because the functions of almost all systems in the body will gradually decline for largely unknown reasons. This decline has a negative impact on physical, mental and social functions. Therefore, old people are at higher risk of chronic non-communicable diseases, such as cardiovascular disease (CVD), diabetes, osteoarthritis, Alzheimer's disease, Parkinson disease, etc. With the rapid increase of the elderly population, it is urgent to improve the healthy life expectancy of old people.

衰老对人类来说是一个自然的、不可抗拒的过程。衰老不是一种疾病，但它是许多疾病的危险因素，因为身体几乎所有系统的功能都由于未知的原因而逐渐衰退。这种衰退会对身体、精神和社会功能产生负面影响。因此，老年人患心血管疾病（CVD）、糖尿病、骨关节炎、阿尔茨海默病（AD）、帕金森病等慢性非传染性疾病的风险较高。随着老年人口的快速增长，提高老年人的健康预期寿命已刻不容缓。

13.1 Physical Fitness and Aging
身体适能与衰老

As we all know, physical activity refers to any energy-consuming movement produced by skeletal muscle, whereas physical fitness is a measurable state of physical functioning, including strength, endurance and flexibility, etc. Exercise is a planned physical activity with the goal of improving physical fitness and health.

我们知道，身体活动是指骨骼肌产生的任何消耗能量的运动，而身体适能是指可测量的身体机能状态，如力量、耐力、柔韧等。运动锻炼是一种以提高身体适能和健康水平为目的的有计划的身体活动。

A person who is physically fit has achieved a physiological state of well-being that allows him or her to successfully meet the demands of daily life or sport performance. The most frequently cited components of physical fitness are divided into two groups: health-related attributes and performance-related skills. There are five health-related components of physical fitness: cardiorespiratory endurance, muscular endurance, muscular strength, flexibility, and body composition. They are important to public health. The skill-related components of physical fitness include agility, coordination, balance, speed, power, and reaction time. Individuals who perform exercises to enhance these components typically have already achieved a certain level of physical fitness, as these skills are required for the performance of most sport activities.

一个身体健康的人已经达到了一种健康的生理状态，使其能够成功地应对日常生活及运动锻炼的需求。身体适能的组成可以分为两类：一类与健康相关，另一类与运动表现相关。5个与健康相关的身体适能指标分别是心肺耐力、肌肉耐力、肌肉力量、柔韧性和身体成分，这些指标对公共健康很重要。与运动表现相关的身体适能指标包括灵敏、协调、平衡、速度、力量和反应时。那些通过锻炼来增强这些身体适能指标的人通常已经达到了一定的水平，因为这些身体适能指标是大多数体育活动所必需的。

As we get older, our physical fitness declines in a roughly linear fashion (Figure 13.1). But physically active people have higher fitness level than physically inactive people at any age; that is why active people and athletes look physiologically younger than inactive people.

随着年龄的增长，身体适能以接近线性的速度降低（图 13.1）。但在任何年龄，经常运动的人的身体适能都比不运动的人要高，这就是为什么经常运动的人比不运动的人在生理上显得更年轻。

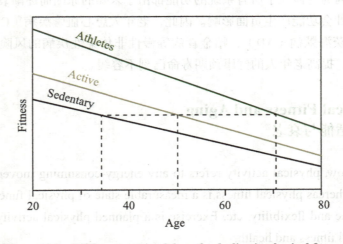

Figure 13.1　Lifelong exercise delays the decline in physical fitness

13.2 Exercise and Healthy Aging and Longevity
运动与增龄健康

As we get older, individuals who are inactive are at increased risk of all-cause mortality, overweight, obesity, type 2 diabetes, colon cancer, poor quality of life, and difficulty living independently. Nevertheless, regular exercise not only delays the usual decline in cardiorespiratory fitness (CRF), muscle mass and muscle strength, slows the progression of neurodegenerative diseases such as dementia and Parkinson disease, but also prevent Alzheimer's disease and dementia.

随着年龄的增长，不爱运动的人全因死亡、超重、肥胖、2 型糖尿病、结肠癌、生活质量差和独立生活困难等的风险增加。有规律的运动锻炼不仅可以延缓心肺耐力（CRF）、肌肉质量和肌肉力量的下降，减缓痴呆、帕金森病等神经退行性疾病的进展，而且还可以预防阿尔茨海默病和老年痴呆。

More physical activity, lower mortality rate. More and more evidence emphasizes that moderate-intensity physical activities, such as brisk walking, have a positive impact on life extension. There are some data indicating that participating in moderate-intensity physical activities shows a trend of lower mortality rate, and the greater the energy expended in vigorous activities, the lower the mortality rate. In contrast, participating in light-intensity physical activities, regardless of energy expenditure, will not reduce mortality rate. Although vigorous activity provides the greatest benefits in terms of longevity, it is not feasible to expect all individuals to be able to perform high-intensity exercise, especially for those who have contraindications. They need proper supervision or expert guidance to avoid injury or overtraining.

更多的身体活动转化为更低的死亡率。越来越多的研究表明中等强度的身体活动，如快走，对延长寿命有积极的影响。有数据表明，参加中等强度的身体活动具有降低死亡率的趋势，在高强度身体活动中，能量消耗越大，死亡率越低。相比之下，从事低强度的身体活动，无论能量消耗如何，都不能降低死亡率。虽然高强度运动在延长寿命方面的益处最大，但期望所有人都能进行高强度运动是不可行的，尤其是对那些有禁忌症的人，他们需要适当的监督或专家的指导，以避免受伤或过度训练。

Research on the association between physical activity and mortality rate has suggested that the introduction of regular exercise even later in life can positively influence longevity. Therefore, efforts to promote physical activity are very important even among middle-aged individuals. It's never too late to start exercising.

对身体活动与死亡率之间关系的研究表明，即使在生命后期进行有规律的锻炼也可以对寿命产生积极的影响。因此，即使是中年人，努力提高身体活动也是重要的。任何时候开始锻炼都不晚。

Chapter 14　Exercise and Body Weight Management

第十四章　运动与体重管理

Human body weight refers to the mass or weight of a person and is measured in kilograms worldwide. The prevalence of overweight and obesity is on a rise globally, especially as the rise in childhood obesity has never been more rapid. It is imperative to have a clear understanding of such complex disease.

体重是指一个人的质量或重量，国际上是以千克（kg）为单位测量的。世界范围内超重和肥胖率正在上升，特别是儿童肥胖的上升速度从未如此之快。必须清楚地了解这一复杂的疾病。

14.1 Body Weight Management
体重管理

In addition to genetic, behavioral, metabolic and hormonal factors, long-term imbalances between energy intake and energy expenditure are the main direct cause influencing the body weight. When calories ingested are more than burned through exercise and normal daily activities, the excess calories are stored primarily in the form of triacylglycerols in adipocytes, followed by body weight gain.

除遗传、行为、代谢和激素外，能量摄入和能量消耗的长期不平衡是影响体重的主要直接原因。当摄入的热量超过运动和日常活动消耗的热量时，多余的热量主要以甘油三酯的形式储存在脂肪细胞中，从而引起体重增加。

Body mass index [BMI = weight (kg)/height(m^2)] is a common tool for estimating body weight (Table 14.1). For most people, BMI provides a reasonable estimate of body fat. However, BMI doesn't directly measure body fat, so some people, such as muscular athletes, may have a BMI in the obesity category even though they don't have excess body fat. Therefore, we need to distinguish the terms of overweight, overfat and obesity. Overweight simply refers to a body weight more than average for the height. Overfat is a term used to describe the condition of body fat exceeding a healthy standard, which is determined by the measuring of percent body fat. Men with 25% or more body fat and women with 32% or more are considered overfat (as well as obese). Obesity refers to the overfat condition that accompanies a host of comorbidities.

体重指数［BMI，BMI= 体重（kg）/ 身高（m²）］是评估体重的常用工具（表 14.1）。对大多数人来说，BMI 适用于评估体脂。然而，BMI 并不是对身体脂肪含量的直接测量。一些人，比如肌肉发达的运动员，即使他们没有多余的身体脂肪，他们的 BMI 也可能属于肥胖。因此，我们需要区分超重、体脂超标和肥胖。超重就是指体重超过了相应身高应有的体重平均值；体脂超标是指身体脂肪含量超过了健康的标准，这是通过测量一个人的身体脂肪的百分比来确定的，体脂含量超过 25% 的男性和超过 32% 的女性被认为是体脂超标；肥胖指的是伴随着许多合并症的体脂超标。

Table 14.1   The Body Weight Classification of Adult According to BMI

Body Weight Classification		BMI Standard		
		WHO	Asian	China
Thin		< 18.5	< 18.5	< 18.5
Normal		18.5–24.9	18.5–22.9	18.5–23.9
Overweight		≥ 25.0	≥ 23.0	≥ 24.0
Obesity	Mild obesity	25.0–29.9	23.0–24.9	24.0–26.9
	Moderate obesity	30.0–34.9	25.0–29.9	27.0–28.9
	Severe obesity	35.0–39.9	≥ 30.0	≥ 29.0
	Extreme obesity	≥ 40.0	–	–

Both being thin and being overweight/obese have negative health risks (Table 14.2). Keeping energy balance to reach and maintain a healthy weight is important for overall health and the prevention and management of many diseases and symptoms.

体重无论是偏瘦还是超重 / 肥胖都有负面的健康风险（表 14.2）。保持能量平衡以达到和保持健康的体重，对整体健康以及预防和控制许多疾病及症状都很重要。

Table 14.2　BMI and Risk of Obesity-Related Disease

Diseases	BMI/kg·(m²)⁻¹			
	<25.0	25.0–<30.0	30.0–35.0	>35.0
Arthritis	1.00	1.56	1.87	2.39
Heart disease	1.00	1.39	1.86	1.67
Diabetes (type 2)	1.00	2.42	3.35	6.16
Gallstones	1.00	1.97	3.30	5.48
Hypertension	1.00	1.92	2.82	3.77
Stroke	1.00	1.53	2.59	1.75

A value of 1.00 equals a standard level of risk, whereas values exceeding 1.00 represents increased risk. For example, a value of 1.87 means that the individual is at an 87% greater level of risk.

14.2 Obesity
肥胖

Obesity is a complex disease involving an excessive amount of body fat, which can be classified as fat cell hypertrophy and fat cell hyperplasia according to the fat cell size and number. Overweight individuals will generally have larger adipocytes than lean individuals without a significant change in the total number. Obese individuals are accompanied by more and larger adipocytes compared with lean individuals (Figure 14.1).

肥胖是一种由体脂含量过多引起的复杂疾病，按脂肪细胞大小和数量可分为脂肪细胞肥大和脂肪细胞增生。在脂肪细胞总量没有明显变化的情况下，超重的人通常比瘦的人有更大的脂肪细胞。与瘦的人相比，肥胖的人会有更多更大的脂肪细胞（图 14.1）。

Obesity is associated with many adverse health outcomes, such as cardiovascular disease, diabetes, high blood pressure and certain cancers (Figure 14.2). According to the location of body fat storage, obesity can also be classified as apple-shaped obesity and pear-shaped obesity. Overweight and obese men tend to distribute their fat around the trunk (apple-shaped obesity) and pear-shaped women tend to distribute fat around the hips and thighs (pear-shaped obesity). The apple-shaped obesity patterns are associated more often with a greater risk of cardiovascular disease and type 2 diabetes compared with the gynoid obesity.

肥胖与许多疾病风险相关，如心血管疾病、糖尿病、高血压和某些癌症（图 14.2）。根据体内脂肪储存的位置，肥胖也可以分为苹果型肥胖和梨型肥胖。超重和肥胖的男性脂肪分布在躯干，属苹果型肥胖，而女性则分布在臀部和大腿，属梨型肥胖。与梨型肥胖相比，苹果型肥胖更容易引发心血管疾病和 2 型糖尿病。

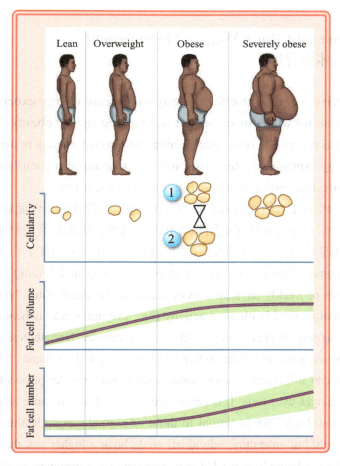

Figure 14.1   The state of fat cells (adipocytes) and adipogenesis in lean and obese individuals

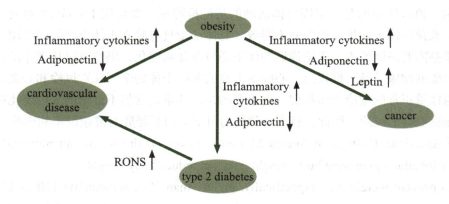

Figure 14.2   The association of obesity and chronic diseases

14.3 Exercise and Body Weight Management
运动与体重管理

Regular exercise is the most effective way to increase energy expenditure, so it is an indispensable weapon for weight management and fighting against obesity. Moderate-intensity continuous training is superior to resistance training and interval training in this regard, because it causes greater energy expenditure. Resistance training programs can contribute to weight loss at rest by positively affecting resting energy expenditure to some extent.

规律的运动是增加能量消耗的最有效的方法，是体重管理和预防肥胖不可缺少的手段。中等强度的持续训练在这方面优于抗阻训练和间歇训练，因为它会消耗更多的能量。抗阻训练计划通过对休息时的能量消耗的持续性积极影响，在一定程度上有助于减轻体重。

The dose-response relationship between physical activity and health (Table 14.3) clarifies how varying amounts of weekly physical activity contribute to health status. Notably, the minimum recommended amount of weekly physical activity (i.e., 150 min/week) is beneficial for health but not effective in managing or preventing weight gain or obesity. Nonetheless, the health benefits of physical activity are generally independent of body weight. This means that individuals who need to lose weight can still receive major health benefits from regular physical activity, no matter how their weight changes over time. It is reported that the risk of all-cause and CVD mortality in obese individuals with high CRF is similar to those of normal weight healthy individuals. What is more, normal-weight but unhealthy individuals could be at a higher risk than obese but healthy individuals. Therefore, relative higher CRF may attenuate the consequences of obesity on health.

身体活动与健康的剂量效应关系（表 14.3）阐明了每周不同的身体活动水平对健康状况的影响。值得注意的是，每周身体活动的最低推荐量（即每周 150 min）对健康有益，但对控制或预防体重增加或肥胖并不奏效。身体活动具有独立于体重之外的健康益处。这意味着那些需要减肥的人，无论他们的体重随时间如何变化，仍然可以从规律的身体活动中获得主要的健康益处。据报道，心肺耐力高的肥胖个体的全因死亡风险和心血管疾病死亡风险与体重正常的健康个体相似。更重要的是，体重正常但不健康的人可能比肥胖但健康的人面临更高的风险。因此，较高心肺耐力可能会减轻肥胖对健康的不利影响。

The American College of Sports Medicine provided the following physical activity guidelines for adults to prevent body weight gain and reduce body weight:

· To prevent weight gain (specifically, greater than 3%), accumulate 150 to 250 min of moderate-intensity or vigorous exercise per week, with an energy expenditure of 1,200 to 2,000 kcal.

· To achieve a clinically significant weight loss of at least 5%, one should accumulate at least 225 min of exercise per week. Weight loss hinges on exercise time. Roughly speaking, every 50 min of exercise per week results in a loss of 1 kg in six months. Thus, a person who exercises

Table 14.3 The dose-response relationship between physical activity and health

Physical Activity Level	Moderate-intensity Activity/week	General Health Benefits	Lifestyle Application
Inactivity	No activity beyond baseline	None	Being inactive is unhealthy
Low	Activity beyond baseline but fewer than 150 min	Some	Low levels of activity are clearly preferable to an inactive lifestyle
Medium	150–300 min	Substantial	Activity at the high end of this range has additional and more extensive health benefits than activity at the low end
High	> 300 min	Additional	There is no identifiable upper limit of activity above which there are no additional health benefits

for 250 min per week will lose 5 kg in six months (solely from exercise).

· To maintain weight after losing weight, it is necessary to accumulate 200 to 300 min of exercise per week. Regular exercise appears to be indispensable for the maintenance of weight loss.

· Combined with moderate dieting, regular physical activity can promote the weight loss. But if people take the severe dieting, the energy intake is lower than resting energy expenditure. The reason probably relates to survival-related metabolic adaptations, which counter the effect of exercise on weight loss .

美国运动医学学会为成年人提供了预防体重增加、减轻体重的身体活动指南：

· 为了防止体重增加（特别是超过 3%），每周应进行 150~250 min 的中等强度或高强度运动，能量消耗为 1,200~2,000 kcal。

· 为了达到至少 5% 的临床显著减肥效果，每周应至少锻炼 225 min。减肥取决于锻炼时间，粗略地说，每周锻炼 50 min，6 个月就能减掉 1 kg。因此，一个人每周锻炼 250 min，6 个月就可以减掉 5 kg（仅仅是运动）。

· 为了在减肥后保持体重，每周应累积进行 200~300 min 的运动锻炼。要想保持减肥效果，定期锻炼是必不可少的。

· 身体活动如果与适度节食相结合，可以促进体重的减轻。如果进行严苛的节食，导致能量摄入低于静息能量消耗，则机体的基础代谢会适应性地降低，进而抵消了运动对减肥的影响。

It's worth mentioning that it is impossible to cause local fat loss (also referred to as spot reduction) by exercising specific parts of the body. If a person has enough exercise to achieve fat loss the whole body fat will be mobilized, no matter which part of the body is involved in the exercise.

需要指出的是，不可能通过锻炼身体特定部位来减少局部脂肪（也称局部减脂）。如果一个人进行充分的运动以达到减肥的目的，那么无论身体的哪个部位参与了运动，全身的脂肪都将被动员。

Chapter 15 Exercise and Chronic Metabolic Diseases

第十五章 运动与慢性代谢性疾病

It is reported that chronic non-communicable diseases, including cardiovascular disease, cancer, diabetes, obesity, metabolic syndrome, osteoporosis, mental disease etc., have become the leading cause of sickness and death worldwide. In addition to obesity, inactive individuals also have higher prevalence of CVD, diabetes, osteoporosis, and mental illness. Regular exercise is a powerful weapon against chronic disease morbidity and mortality.

据报道，慢性非传染性疾病，包括心血管疾病、癌症、糖尿病、肥胖、代谢综合征、骨质疏松症、精神疾病等已成为全球致病和死亡的首要原因。除了肥胖，不爱运动的人患心血管疾病、糖尿病、骨质疏松症和精神疾病的概率也较高。经常运动是降低慢性病发病率和死亡率的有效手段。

15.1 Exercise and Cardiovascular Disease
运动与心血管疾病

Cardiovascular disease (CVD) is a broad term encompassing various conditions, including coronary artery disease, stroke, angina, myocardial infarction (or heart attack), heart failure, and heart arrhythmia. And CVD is the leading cause of morbidity and mortality worldwide. The Major causes of CVD include atherosclerosis and hypertension. Most CVD can be prevented by a healthy diet, avoiding tobacco smoking, limiting alcohol consumption, and regular exercise.

心血管疾病是循环系统疾病的统称，包括冠状动脉疾病、中风、心绞痛、心肌梗死、心力衰竭和心律失常等多种疾病，是全球发病率和死亡率均排名第一的疾病。心血管疾病的主要病因包括动脉粥样硬化和高血压。大多数心血管疾病可以通过健康饮食、戒烟、限制酒精摄入和定期运动来预防。

Epidemiological studies have shown that regular physical activity is associated with reduced CVD morbidity and mortality. Moderate-intensity continuous training (MICT), resistance training, and interval training seem to be effective ways of lowering CVD risk. For example, endurance and resistance training can reduce the risk of atherosclerosis by decreasing plasma triacylglycerols (Figure 15.1), total cholesterol and LDL cholesterol, and increasing HDL cholesterol. In addition, the increase in blood flow and pressure associated with exercise can lead to structural and functional adaptations of the vascular wall, thereby reducing the risk of atherosclerosis.

流行病学研究表明，经常性的运动与心血管疾病的低发病率和低死亡率相关。中等强度的持续训练、抗阻训练和间歇训练是降低心血管疾病风险的有效手段。例如，耐力训练和抗阻训练可以通过降低血浆甘油三酯（图 15.1）、总胆固醇、低密度脂蛋白胆固醇和增加高密度脂蛋白胆固醇来降低动脉粥样硬化的风险。此外，伴随运动而来的血流量和压力增加会导致血管壁的结构和功能的适应性变化，从而降低动脉粥样硬化的风险。

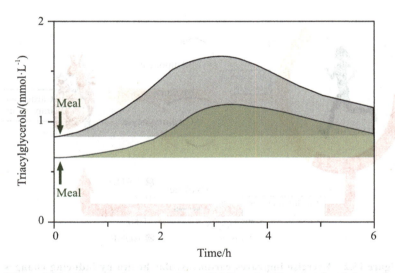

Figure 15.1　Exercise lowers postprandial lipemia. Plasma triacylglycerol concentration rises after we consume a meal and remains elevated for several hours until dietary lipids are delivered to the tissues. If we have exercise before a meal, both the fasting concentration (at 0 h) and the postprandial concentration are lower (colored line) compared with the values in the absence of previous exercise (black line). In addition, the so-called incremental area under the curve (shading) is smaller than post exercise

Exercise improves oxygen delivery throughout the body by promoting vasodilation and angiogenesis (Figure 15.2 A). Exercise increases mitochondrial biogenesis in adipocytes, skeletal muscle myotubes, and cardiomyocytes (Figure 15.2 B). Exercise causes a long-term anti-inflammatory effect (which is inversely related to the increased inflammation typically seemed in CVD and obesity). Myokines released from skeletal muscle during physical exercise partially mediate these anti-inflammatory effects and promote inter-tissue cross talk to mediate further cardiovascular benefits (Figure 15.2 C).

运动可以通过促进血管舒张和血管生成来提高全身的氧气输送量（图 15.2 A）。运动可增加脂肪细胞、骨骼肌肌管和心肌细胞的线粒体合成（图 15.2 B）。运动会引起长期的抗炎效果（与心血管疾病和肥胖发生的典型的炎症反应增加负相关）。运动过程中从骨骼肌释放的肌激素部分介导了这些抗炎作用，并促进组织间的交互作用，进而带来更多的心血管益处（图 15.2 C）。

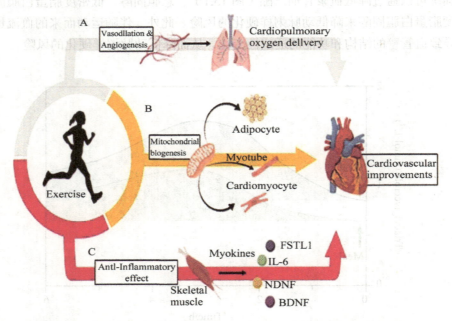

Figure 15.2　Exercise improves cardiovascular health by inducing changes in oxygen delivery, vasculature, peripheral tissues, and inflammation

15.2 Exercise and Diabetes
运动与糖尿病

Diabetes is a hyperglycemia disease caused by insulin deficiency or malfunction of hormone signaling pathways. Diabetes is classified into 2 types according to the cause. Type 1 diabetes (T1D) is primarily due to autoimmune destruction of β cells in the pancreas, which results in inability of the organ to secrete insulin. In most cases, T1D appears early in life, which is why it is often characterized as juvenile. It is also referred to as insulin-dependent diabetes mellitus. The disease is treated with regular insulin injections to replace the missing natural hormone. Type 2 diabetes (T2D) is caused by insulin resistance (Figure 15.3). Although the pancreas produces insulin, the hormone is incapable of regulating the blood glucose levels. T2D is also named as insulin-resistant diabetes, non-insulin-dependent diabetes mellitus, and adult-onset diabetes, because it usually appears later in life.

　　糖尿病是一种因胰岛素缺乏或胰岛素信号转导通路功能障碍而导致高血糖症状的疾病。根据病因，糖尿病分为 1 型糖尿病和 2 型糖尿病两类。1 型糖尿病主要是由于胰腺细胞的自身免疫破坏，导致该器官无法分泌胰岛素。在大多数情况下，1 型糖尿病在生命的早期就出现了，这就是为什么它常常被认为是青少年型糖尿病的原因。1 型糖尿病也称为胰岛素依赖型糖尿病。治疗 1 型糖尿病需要定期注射胰岛素，以补充体内缺失的天然激素。2 型糖尿病是由胰岛素抵抗引起的（图 15.3），虽然胰腺能够产生胰岛素，但胰岛素无法调节血糖水平。2 型糖尿病又称为胰岛素抵抗型糖尿病或非胰岛素依赖型糖尿病，也称为成人型糖尿病，因为它通常出现在生命的后期。

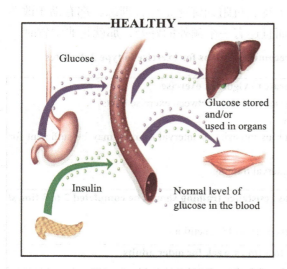 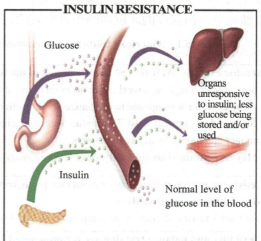

Figure 15.3　Insulin resistance

Hyperglycemia occurs when glucose is removed from the circulation at a reduced rate but appears in the circulation at an increased rate. The reduced disappearance rate is due to the failure of GLUT4 to translocate to the plasma membrane from its intracellular reservoir in muscle fibers and adipocytes. The increased appearance rate is due to excessive glucose production in the liver, since glycogenolysis and gluconeogenesis are not restrained in the absence of insulin or insulin resistance.

高血糖的发生是因为葡萄糖从循环中消失的速度降低，而在循环中出现的速度增加。前者是由于 GLUT4 不能从肌纤维和脂肪细胞的细胞内储藏库转移到质膜；而循环中葡萄糖出现率增加是因为在胰岛素缺乏或胰岛素抵抗的情况下，糖原分解和糖异生不受限制，导致肝脏分解出过多的葡萄糖。

Exercise is typically one of the preferred management strategies advising for patients with type 2 diabetes (Table 15.1). Exercise leads to increased migration of GLUT4 from intracellular vesicles to the plasma membrane of the active muscle fibers, and increases the muscle GLUT4 content. Exercise improves insulin secretion from the pancreas, increases the insulin sensitivity of skeletal muscle, liver, and adipose tissue, and strengthens the "organ crosstalk" (Figure 15.4). Exercise training, whether aerobic or resistance training or a combination, facilitates improved glucose regulation. High-intensity interval training is also effective and it has the added benefit of saving time.

运动通常是 2 型糖尿病患者的首要管理策略之一（表 15.1）。运动可促使 GLUT4 从细胞内囊泡迁移到运动肌纤维的质膜，增加肌肉中的 GLUT4 含量。运动可以改善胰腺的胰岛素分泌，从而增加骨骼肌、肝脏和脂肪组织的胰岛素敏感性，并增强组织器官间的交互作用（图 15.4）。运动训练，无论是有氧训练、抗阻训练还是综合训练，都有助于改善血糖调节。高强度的间歇训练也是有效的，而且还有一个额外的好处，那就是非常省时。

Table 15.1　American Diabetes Association recommendations for exercise in type 2 diabetes

Aerobic exercise: At least 150 minutes/week of moderate to vigorous exercise
• Spread over 3 to 7 days/week, with no more than 2 consecutive days between exercise bouts
• Daily exercise is suggested to maximize insulin action
• Shorter durations (at least 75 minutes/week) of vigorous-intensity or interval training may be sufficient for younger and more physically fit patients
• May be performed continuously, or as high-intensity interval training
Resistance exercise: Progressive moderate to vigorous resistance training should be completed 2 to 3 times/week on nonconsecutive days
• At least 8 to 10 exercises, with completion of 1 to 3 sets of 10 to 15 repetitions
Flexibility and balance training are recommended 2 to 3 times/week for older adults
Participation in supervised training programs is recommended to maximize health benefits of exercise in type 2 diabetes

15.3 Exercise and Osteoporosis
运动与骨质疏松症

Osteoporosis is a disease characterized by abnormal low bone mineral density (BMD), which reduces bone strength and increases the risk of fractures, even with minor stress. Osteoporosis

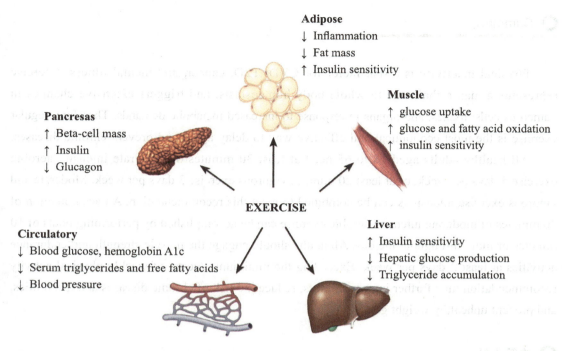

Adipose
↓ Inflammation
↓ Fat mass
↑ Insulin sensitivity

Muscle
↑ glucose uptake
↑ glucose and fatty acid oxidation
↑ insulin sensitivity

Pancresas
↑ Beta-cell mass
↑ Insulin
↓ Glucagon

EXERCISE

Circulatory
↓ Blood glucose, hemoglobin A1c
↓ Serum triglycerides and free fatty acids
↓ Blood pressure

Liver
↑ Insulin sensitivity
↓ Hepatic glucose production
↓ Triglyceride accumulation

Figure 15.4   Tissue-specific metabolic effects of exercise in patients with type 2 diabetes

is more prevalent in women than in men because women's BMD lose seems more rapid after the age of 30. It is particularly prevalent after menopause, primarily due to a decline in estrogen levels.

骨质疏松症是一种以骨矿物质密度（BMD）异常低为特征的疾病，它会降低骨强度，增加骨折的风险，即使仅仅是受到轻微的压力也是如此。女性患骨质疏松症的几率高于男性，因为女性在 30 岁后骨密度的下降更快。绝经后尤其普遍，主要原因是雌激素水平下降。

Regular exercise, including resistance training or weight loading exercise, elicits a BMD increase and reduces bone fracture rates in patients with osteoporosis. In addition, balance and flexibility training help to prevent falls, especially in elderly adults.

有规律的运动，包括抗阻训练或负重运动，可以促进骨密度的增加，降低骨质疏松症患者的骨折发生率。此外，平衡和柔韧训练，也有助于防止老年人摔倒。

Accumulation of maximum BMD in early adulthood is crucial for preventing osteoporosis in later life, and this accumulation may be achieved through regular exercise in childhood and adolescence. It is remarkable that physically active children and adolescents have 10% to 20% higher BMD than their inactive counterparts.

在成年早期积累最大的骨密度对于预防晚年骨质疏松症至关重要，这种积累可以通过在幼儿期和青春期进行规律的运动来实现。值得一提的是，经常运动的儿童和青少年的骨密度比不运动的同龄人高出 10%~20%。

Summary

Physical inactivity is a risk factor for CVD, T2D, cancer, and mental illness. Exercise represents a major challenge to whole-body homeostasis, and triggers extensive changes in numerous cells, tissues, and organs in response to increased metabolic demands. Therefore, regular exercise is the most economical and effective way to delay aging and prevent chronic diseases.

All healthy adults aged 18 to 65 need at least 30 minutes of moderate intensity aerobic exercise 5 days per week, or at least 20 minutes vigorous exercise 3 days per week. Moderate and vigorous exercise intensities can be combined to meet this recommendation. An accumulation of 30 minutes of moderate intensity aerobic exercise can be accomplished by performing bouts of 10 minutes or more throughout the day. All adults should engage the muscle strength and endurance activities at least 2 days per week. Exceeding the minimum amount of weekly physical activity recommendation may further improve fitness, reduce the risk of chronic diseases and disabilities, and prevent unhealthy weight gain.

本篇小结

身体活动不足是心血管疾病、2 型糖尿病、癌症和精神疾病的危险因素。运动对全身内稳态提出重大挑战，并且为了响应增加的代谢需求，在诸多细胞、组织和器官中触发广泛的变化。因此，规律运动是延缓衰老、预防慢性疾病最经济有效的方法。

所有 18~65 岁的健康成年人都需要进行每周 5 次、每次至少 30 min 的中等强度有氧运动，或每周 3 次、每次至少 20 min 的高强度运动。中等强度和高强度的运动可以结合起来进行以满足这一建议。通过全天进行多次 10 min 或更长时间的运动，可以累积完成 30 min 中等强度的有氧运动。所有成年人每周至少有两天要进行肌肉力量和耐力活动。超过每周建议的最低运动量，可进一步改善健康状况，降低慢性病和残疾的风险，预防不健康的体重增加。

References

参考文献

[1] MOUGIOS V. Exercise biochemistry [M]. Champaign, IL: Human Kinetics, 2020.

[2] MCARDLE W D, KATCH F I, KATCH V L. Exercise physiolgy: nutrition, energy, and human performance[M]. 7th ed. Philadelphia: Lippincott Williams & Wilkins, 2010.

[3] PORCARI J P, BRYANT C X, COMANA F. Exercise physiology[M]. Philadelphia: F.A.Davis, 2015.

[4] MACLAREN D, MORTON J.Biochemistry for sport and exercise metabolism[M]. Hoboken: John Wiley & Sons, Ltd, 2012.

[5] LIEBERMAN M, PEET A. Marks' essentials of medical biochemistry: a clinical approach[M]. 2nd ed. Philadelphia: Lippincott Williams & Wilkins, 2015.

[6] FERRIER D R. Biochemistry[M]. 7th ed. Philadelphia: Wolters Kluwer, 2017.

Terms
专业术语

英文名称	英文缩写	中文名称
A		
abdominal adipose tissue		腹部脂肪组织
acute exercise		急性运动
adenylate kinase	**AK**	腺苷酸激酶
aerobic exercise		有氧运动
aerobic pathway		有氧通路
aerobic system		有氧系统
amylopectin		支链淀粉
amylose		直链淀粉
anabolism		合成代谢
anaerobic exercise		无氧运动
anaerobic pathway		无氧通路
anaerobic threshold	AT	无氧阈
anerobic glycolysis		无氧糖酵解
ATP-ADP cycle		ATP–ADP 循环
ATP-phosphagen system		ATP– 磷酸原系统

英文名称	英文缩写	中文名称
B		
blood glucose		血糖
blood sugar		血糖
bone mineral density	BMD	骨密度
branched chain amino acid	BCAA	支链氨基酸
brown adipose tissue	BAT	棕色脂肪组织
β-oxidation		β 氧化
C		
carbohydrate loading		糖原负荷
cardiovascular disease	CVD	心血管疾病
cardiorespiratory fitness	CRF	心肺适能 / 心肺耐力
catabolism		分解代谢
central fatigue		中枢疲劳
chronic non-communicable disease		慢性非传染性疾病
chylomicron	CM	乳糜微粒
citric acid cycle		柠檬酸循环
coenzyme		辅酶
complete protein		完全蛋白质
concurrent effect		同时作用
concurrent training	CT	同步训练
Cori cycle		柯氏循环
creatine		肌酸
creatine kinase	CK	肌酸激酶
D		
diabetes	DB	糖尿病
direct energy source		直接能源
E		
endergonic reaction		吸能反应
endurance exercise		耐力运动
energy continuum		连续能区

英文名称	英文缩写	中文名称
energy metabolism		能量代谢
essential amino acid	EAA	必需氨基酸
essential fatty acid	EFA	必需脂肪酸
exercise		运动
exercise adaptation		运动适应
exercise metabolism		运动代谢
exercise training		运动训练
exergonic reaction		放能反应
extracellular fluid		细胞外液
F		
fatigue		疲劳
fat-soluble vitamin		脂溶性维生素
fatty acid	FA	脂肪酸
fiber		纤维
fructose		果糖
G		
galactose		半乳糖
gluconeogenesis		糖异生
glucose		葡萄糖
glucose transporter 4	GLUT4	葡萄糖转运蛋白 4
glucose-alanine cycle		葡萄糖 – 丙氨酸循环
glycemic index	GI	升糖指数
glycerol		甘油
glycogen		糖原
glycogenesis		糖原生成
glycogenolysis		糖原分解
H		
heart rate	HR	心率
high-density lipoprotein	HDL	高密度脂蛋白
high-energy phosphate bonds		高能磷酸键

英文名称	英文缩写	中文名称
high-energy phosphate compounds		高能磷酸化合物
high-intensity exercise	HIE	高强度运动
high-intensity interval training	HIIT	高强度间歇训练
hypoglycemia		低血糖
I		
immediate and short-term energy system		即时和短期能源系统
incomplete protein		不完全蛋白质
indirect energy source		间接能源
insulin resistance		胰岛素阻抗
interference effect		干扰作用
intracellular fluid		细胞内液
K		
ketogenic diet	KD	生酮饮食
L		
lactate system		乳酸系统
lactate threshold	LT	乳酸阈值
lactose		乳糖
lactose intolerance		乳糖不耐症
lipid		脂质
lipoprotein		脂蛋白
liver glycogen		肝糖原
long-chain triacylglycerols	LCT	长链甘油三酯
long-term energy system		长期能源系统
long-term exercise		长期运动
low-carbohydrate high-fat diet	LCHF	低碳水化合物高脂饮食
low-density lipoprotein	LDL	低密度脂蛋白
M		
macronutrient		大量营养素
major mineral		主要矿物质
maltose		麦芽糖

英文名称	英文缩写	中文名称
maximum fat oxidation	MFO	最大脂肪氧化
maximum heart rate	HRmax	最大心率
maximum rate of oxygen uptake	$\dot{V}O_2max$	最大摄氧量
medium-chain triacylglycerol	MCT	中链甘油三酯
metabolic control		代谢调控
metabolic equivalent	MET	代谢当量
metabolism		新陈代谢
metallic mineral		金属矿物质
micronutrient		微量营养素
minor mineral		次要矿物质
moderate-intensity continuous training	MICT	中等强度持续训练
monosaccharide		单糖
monounsaturated fatty acid	MUFA	单不饱和脂肪酸
movement fitness		健身运动
muscle glycogen		肌肉糖原
muscle hypertrophy		肌肥大
N		
nicotinamide adenine dinucleotide	NAD	烟酰胺腺嘌呤二核苷酸
non-essential amino acid		非必需氨基酸
non-metallic mineral		非金属矿物质
nutrition		营养
O		
obesity		肥胖
oligosaccharide		寡糖
one-repetition maximum	1RM	一次最大反复
osteoporosis		骨质疏松症
oxidative phosphorylation		氧化磷酸化
P		
perceived fatigue		感知疲劳
performance fatigue		表现疲劳

英文名称	英文缩写	中文名称
peripheral fatigue		外周疲劳
phosphatidic acid		磷脂酸
phosphocreatine	PCr	磷酸肌酸
phospholipid		磷脂
physical activity	PA	体力活动
physical fitness		身体适能
polysaccharide		多糖
polyunsaturated fatty acid	PUFA	多不饱和脂肪酸
R		
rating of perceived exertion	RPE	运动自觉量表
reduced nicotinamide adenine dinucleotide	NADH	还原型烟酰胺腺嘌呤二核苷酸
resistance exercise		阻力运动
ribose		核糖
S		
saccharide		糖类
short-term exercise		短期运动
sphingomyelin		鞘磷脂
sprint interval training	SIT	冲刺间歇训练
sprint exercise		冲刺运动
starch		淀粉
steroid		类固醇
subcutaneous adipose tissue		皮下脂肪组织
substrate-level phosphorylation		底物水平磷酸化
sucrose		蔗糖
T		
trace mineral		微量矿物质
training adaptation		训练适应
triacylglycerol	TAGs	甘油三酯
tricarboxylic acid cycle	TCA cycle	三羧酸循环
type 1 diabetes	T1D	1 型糖尿病

英文名称	英文缩写	中文名称
type 2 diabetes	T2D	2 型糖尿病
U		
unsaturated fatty acid		不饱和脂肪酸
V		
very low density lipoprotein	VLDL	极低密度脂蛋白
visceral adipose tissue		内脏脂肪组织
W		
water-soluble vitamin		水溶性维生素
white adipose tissue	WAT	白色脂肪组织
white fat		白色脂肪